KIERKEGAARD

AND THE CRISIS OF FAITH

KIERKEGAARD

AND THE

CRISIS OF FAITH

An Introduction to his Thought

———

GEORGE PATTISON

First published in Great Britain 1997
Society for Promoting Christian Knowledge
Holy Trinity Church
Marylebone Road
London NW1 4DU

British Library Cataloguing-in-Publication Data
A catalogue record of this book is available from
the British Library

ISBN 0-281-05070-8

Typeset by Wilmaset Ltd, Birkenhead, Wirral
Printed in Great Britain by
The Cromwell Press, Melksham, Wiltshire

For Charlotte, Neil and Beth, so they can read what I've been doing all these years.

There is a bird called the stormy-petrel,
and that is what I am, when in a generation
storms begin to gather, individuals of my
type appear.

Søren Kierkegaard, tr. A. Dru.

CONTENTS

PREFACE

AT THE TIME when I became seriously involved in studying Kierkegaard in the early to mid-1980s, it soon became clear that this was not a
clever career move. Even though many in Europe and America con-
tinued to regard him as a major, indeed a central, figure of the modern
tradition, he had never found whole-hearted acceptance in Britain.
Perhaps this is hardly surprising, given a national propensity for the *via
media* and the principle of both-and: what could we make of a thinker
whose life-principle was either-or? Even the interest that came about
through his association with existentialism and dialectical theology
had, in any case, died out by then, as these movements themselves
receded into history. To be sure, there were solitary figures holding out
in the outposts of theology and literature and keeping the flame alive,
but by and large owning up to an all-consuming passion for Kierkegaard's thought was to become guilty by association and to be regarded
as being almost as odd as the man himself. Theology at least had found
other, more robust topics and, for those on the left, individualism (and
who was Kierkegaard if not an individualist?) was an uncomfortable
topic in a period when political individualism was rending the fabric of
national life.

Times change, however, and the 1990s have seen a very different
picture. Apart from my own *Kierkegaard: The Aesthetic and the
Religious* there have been a succession of academic studies produced
by scholars working in Britain: Harvie Ferguson, David Law, Roger
Poole, Anthony Rudd, Michael Weston and, most recently, introduc-
tory studies by Peter Vardy and Julia Watkin. There are not a few PhDs
in progress or recently completed which will doubtless lead to further
publications, not to mention the many scholars in theology, philosophy
and literary studies for whom Kierkegaard is a significant partner-in-
dialogue. Indeed, there is now a Søren Kierkegaard Society of the
United Kingdom and (perhaps to cap it all) he has played a leading role
in a recent novel, *Therapy*, by David Lodge. As in Germany in the
1920s or France in the 1940s, he is in grave danger of becoming trendy!

What justification can there be, therefore, for yet another book about
him? What is there left to say?

It is true: a great deal has been written about this man, about his life, his thought, his writing. But achieving a certain trendiness in the realms of academic discourse cannot be the end of the matter. Kierkegaard, whatever else he was as a writer, did not write primarily for an academic readership. In fact, he spoke scornfully of the day when professors would make a living out of writing about him. Without wishing to define too closely the unifying aim of his authorship, we can at least say that he wrote to provoke existential engagement with crucial situations in life and that, for him, that meant a provocation in the direction of ethical and religious concern. Time of course does not stand still, and Kierkegaard's place and time are distant from our own. But not that distant. This book is written in the conviction that the fundamental dynamics of religion in the situation of modernity are still active in our contemporary world. I do not regard the advent of postmodernity as marking a radical break with this situation but as heightening certain elements or rhythms within it. Kierkegaard may not be right about everything (I'm sure he isn't), but there is much that remains contemporary and even pressing in the questions with which his writing confronts us, questions such as what it is to be religious in a post-traditional, post-hierarchical, and, yes, a post-Christian society.

Because this is a book for the non-specialist, I have tried to avoid too cumbersome an apparatus, and have tried to keep notes to a minimum. Quotations from Kierkegaard's published writings are my own translations from the third Danish edition of his collected works. However, because relatively few readers will have access to the original I have given references to the relevant pages of the current standard English translations of his work, mostly to the complete edition of his published works, *Kierkegaard's Writings*, being produced by the Princeton University Press under the editorship of Howard V. and Edna H. Hong. Where particular volumes have not yet appeared in this series I have referred to older English translations. The abbreviations for these texts are given on pp. xi–xii. Quotations from the voluminous journals and papers are taken from the six-volume edition prepared by H. V. and E. H. Hong. The Hongs have numbered the journal entries to run continuously through all six volumes. These references are also given in the text: JP (= Journals and Papers) followed by the entry number in the Hongs' numbering. On occasion I have had to use material not included in the Hongs' translation. I have then used the Danish edition of the journals (*Papirer*) and given the reference in the standard form, for example, Pap. (= Papirer) I (= vol. no.) C (= subdivision within volume) 42 (entry no. within subdivision).

List of Abbreviations to Kierkegaard's Works

CA   *The Concept of Anxiety*, Princeton University Press, 1980.

CD   *Christian Discourses*, including *The Lilies of the Field and the Birds of the Air* and *Three Discourses at the Communion on Fridays*, Oxford University Press, 1940.

CI   *The Concept of Irony together with 'Notes on Schelling's Berlin Lectures'*, Princeton University Press, 1989.

Cor   *The Corsair Affair*, Princeton University Press, 1982.

CUP   *Concluding Unscientific Postscript*, Princeton University Press, 1992.

EO   *Either/Or*, Princeton University Press, 1987.

EPW   *Early Polemical Writings*, Princeton University Press, 1990.

EUD   *Eighteen Upbuilding Discourses*, Princeton University Press, 1990.

FSE/JY   *For Self-Examination and Judge for Yourself*, Princeton University Press, 1990.

FT/R   *Fear and Trembling and Repetition*, Princeton University Press, 1983.

JP   *Søren Kierkegaard's Journals and Papers*, ed. and tr. Howard V. Hong and Edna H. Hong, assisted by Gregor Malantschuk; Bloomington, Indiana University Press, 1: 1967; 2: 1970; 3 and 4: 1975; 5–7: 1978.

KAUC   *Kierkegaard's Attack upon 'Christendom', 1854–1855*, Princeton University Press, 1944.

LD   *Letters and Documents*, Princeton University Press, 1978.

PA   *The Present Age*, Oxford University Press, 1940.

Pap.   *Søren Kierkegaard's Papirer*, ed. P. A. Heiberg, V. Kuhr and E. Torsting, 2nd edn with Niels Thulstrup, 13 vols, Copenhagen, 1968–70; index by N.-J. Cappelørn, 3 vols, Copenhagen, Gyldendal, 1975–8.

PC   *Practice in Christianity*, Princeton University Press, 1991.

PF/JC   *Philosophical Fragments and Johannes Climacus*, Princeton University Press, 1985.

PV   *The Point of View for My Work as an Author*, including the appendix ' "The Single Individual" Two "Notes" Concerning My Work as an Author' and 'On My Work as an Author', Oxford University Press, 1939.

SLW   *Stages on Life's Way*, Princeton University Press, 1988.

SUD   *The Sickness unto Death*, Princeton University Press, 1980.

TA   *Two Ages: The Age of Revolution and the Present Age. A Literary Review*, Princeton University Press, 1978.

UDVS   *Upbuilding Discourses in Various Spirits*, Princeton University Press, 1993.

WL   *Works of Love*, Princeton University Press, 1995.

Acknowledgements

As this work reflects an interpretation of Kierkegaard arrived at over a number of years, I am well aware that I owe debts to my family, to innumerable friends, colleagues and students (categories that constantly blur into one another) as well as to institutions that have provided invitations, grants, time off, etc., and thereby helped me get thus far in studying Kierkegaard. Rather than attempt a complete list of those to whom I am so indebted, let me thank all, generally, in one large but inadequate gesture of thanks.

I am grateful to the Indiana University Press for permission to reproduce extracts from Howard and Edna Hong (tr. and ed.), *Søren Kierkegaard's Journals and Papers*, Volumes 1–6, Bloomington, 1967–78.

ONE

KIERKEGAARD AND THE CRISIS OF FAITH

———

IN THE TELEVISION series *The Sea of Faith* the radical theologian Don Cupitt described the nineteenth-century Danish writer Søren Aabye Kierkegaard (1813–55) as 'the most important modern Christian writer'.[1] Ludwig Wittgenstein is said to have referred to him in similar terms as 'by far the most profound thinker of the last century. Kierkegaard was a saint',[2] while Karl Barth, probably the most influential theologian of the twentieth century, could place him on a par with such figures as Abraham, Jeremiah, Paul and Luther. In fact, the list of philosophers, theologians, writers and artists who owe an acknowledged debt to him reads like a *Who's Who* of Western culture over the last hundred years. But despite his considerable influence upon many branches of twentieth-century thought, Kierkegaard fits but awkwardly into any canon of religious, philosophical or literary classics. This is especially true in Britain. Why?

To begin with, it is notorious that the sort of philosophical approach with which Kierkegaard is usually identified (existentialism), was never entirely accepted by the Anglo-Saxon philosophical community with its roots in empiricism and linguistic analysis and its focus on matters of science and logic rather than on culture and religion. Existentialism spoke a different language and addressed different questions. Whereas Kierkegaard sought to define the religious significance of anxiety, despair and nothingness, philosophers of the Anglo-Saxon tradition were more concerned to demonstrate that all such talk was unverifiable, unfalsifiable and therefore, no matter how emotionally expressive, philosophically vacuous. Even when existentialism dominated the continental scene, it remained, from the British (and to a lesser extent, from the American) point of view, a storm on a distant horizon. We, it seemed, were to be spared the sudden lightning flashes of anguished freedom which seared the darker European skies. Somewhat belatedly, theology took up some of the existentialists' concerns, notably in John Robinson's *Honest to God* and the 'death of God' theology of the 1960s. Many of the reactions to this style of theologizing, however, simply underlined the point that the emphases of existentialism were, in several senses, foreign to Anglo-Saxon attitudes. One irate colonel summed up the feelings of many when he referred to Robinson's sources as 'alien agnostics'. One of these 'alien agnostics', the German-American theologian Paul Tillich, was himself aware of this intellectual gulf as he observed that

> England is the only European country in which the Existential problem of finding a new meaning for life had no significance, because there positivism and the religious tradition lived on side by side, united by a social conformism which prevented radical questions of the meaning of human 'Existence'. It is important to note that the one country without an Existential philosophy is that in which during the period from 1830 to 1930 the religious tradition remained strongest. This illustrates the dependence of the Existential philosophy on the problems created by the breakdown of the religious tradition on the European continent.[3]

Although some may feel that our recent history has scarcely been as placid as Tillich suggests, the point he is making has been made in much the same terms by many of those critics of existentialism who regard it as little more than a highly sophisticated expression of postwar blues.

In any case, the post-war heyday of existentialism is long past, and it has suffered a substantial diminution of influence even in its continental heartlands. When Jean-Paul Sartre died in 1980, most commentators agreed that existentialism had predeceased its best-known representative.

Even in theology, often a good decade behind the secular world in its intellectual trends, the 1970s brought about the complete eclipse of existentialism as a living influence, as the focus of theological enquiry moved from the search for personal authenticity to the more 'objective' concerns of politics, sociology and methodology. In the Church, as in the world, existentialism became a matter of historical interest rather than of contemporary relevance, and it was hard to see how theologians such as Bultmann and Robinson could have spoken of the dialogue with existentialism as being of ultimate theological concern.

Assuming the association of Kierkegaard with existentialism to be at least in some measure justified, it is clear that such a climate would work against any widespread enthusiasm for his work. Possibly the wheel has turned again, in that the advent of postmodernism (whatever that means) seems to offer important connections with aspects of Kierkegaard's work – but there are, of course, many for whom 'postmodernism' carries similar negative connotations to existentialism: for such critics both are little more than expressions of the relativism, nihilism and stylistic obscurity that are endemic in post-Hegelian European philosophy.

The problem is heightened by factors peculiar to Kierkegaard's work that make it in certain respects considerably more daunting than that of a Sartre, a Jaspers or a Tillich. Not only does he share what Anglo-Saxon philosophers might see as their quasi-mystical philosophical vocabulary, but his writings present us with quite singular literary problems. Kierkegaard was a writer for whom communication was just as much an act of self-concealment as of self-revelation, and he confronts us again and again with deliberate ambiguity. He set out to repel as well as to attract his reader, and no one can be considered a serious reader of his work who has not at some time or other felt the scandal of this repulsive element. There are two distinct but closely connected factors, which are worth briefly examining in this context.

The first concerns the forbidding psychological landscape of Kierkegaard's work. His childhood imbued him with a profound ambivalence towards the body and, especially, towards sexuality. Although he could celebrate the beauties both of eroticism and of married love, he could also indulge an almost Manichean disgust of sexuality and, indeed, the whole biological dimension of life. In this respect it is no accident that his final attack on established Christendom focused repeatedly on issues of marriage, baptism and the family.

The feeling that his writing about such matters has an almost obsessive quality was already found among his contemporaries. Writing of *Guilty? – Not Guilty?* (a part of the larger work *Stages on Life's Way*), in which Kierkegaard obliquely revealed something of his own inner anguish, a contemporary reviewer, describing the author as a 'dialectical executioner', wrote of the 'hero' that

> Here one meets a masculine individual who has lost everything that constitutes personality. Feeling, understanding, will, resolution, action, backbone, nerve and muscle-power – all are dissolved in a dialectic, a barren dialectic that swirls around an indefinite center ... until it eventually, slowly vanishes. (Cor, p. 101)

Even such a dedicated admirer of Kierkegaard as his translator and hagiographer Walter Lowrie could say of this part of the *Stages* that he 'heartily' wished it had never been written. 'I am tired of reading it all', he wrote, 'and find it still more tiresome to translate it.'[4] Pierre Mesnard felt that it read like a transcript from the psycho-analyst's couch.[5] As to what it revealed, the psycho-analyst Rudolph Friedman saw in the imaginative account of Abraham and Isaac in *Fear and Trembling* an unconscious exposure of the inner springs of what he described as Kierkegaard's schizoid personality:

> Behind the mask of literary art, the hidden wish emerges into consciousness ... Perverted, degenerate love and death, murder and incestuous homosexuality merge as the mountain spring of the instinctive Eros gushes forth.[6]

Of course, no psycho-analytic account of any literary work is going to make pleasant reading, but for those whose attitudes towards sexuality are post-Freudian and post-1960s, such a complex of repression and obsession is hardly likely to prove attractive. It is precisely the Victorian syndrome from which we see ourselves as having been liberated.

The ambivalent conjunction of revelation and concealment in Kierkegaard's work is not, however, just a product of his psychological situation. It is also (and many would say more importantly) connected with his conscious and deliberate strategy of 'indirect communication'. His reasons for adopting such a strategy are – at least at the conscious level – rooted in two very sensitive pedagogical insights. Firstly, he saw that the teacher (and in terms of Kierkegaard's own work this means above all the teacher of religion in the modern world) cannot simply catechize the learner 'from above' but must be prepared to meet him where he is.

> For in truth to be able to help another person, I must understand more than him – but nevertheless first and foremost also understand what he understands. If I do not do that then my superior knowledge does not help him at all. If, nevertheless, I assert my superior knowledge, then it is because I am vain or proud, for basically instead of helping him I essentially want to be admired by him. But all true help begins with an act of humility; the helper must first humble himself under the one he wants to help, and therewith understand that to help is not to command but to serve... (PV, pp. 27–8)

The Christian writer must therefore begin by sympathetically entering into and portraying the very position from which, in the long term, he is seeking to liberate his readers. Kierkegaard, therefore, begins by presenting in some detail the 'aesthetic' attitude which he regards as the typical attitude of modern bourgeois society in order to expose its inner contradictions and so lure the reader on to a confrontation with Christianity as an alternative stance towards life that is worth taking seriously. Such a confrontation can never, in his view, be achieved simply by denouncing the shortcomings of the non-Christian world and proclaiming the virtues of faith. The Christian communicator must enter into the inner situation of those to whom he is concerned to communicate and, in doing so, will conceal his identity and purpose behind an incognito that is effective only to the extent that it is impenetrable.

Secondly, the indirect method aims to preserve the freedom and responsibility of the learner in the teacher-pupil relationship. If Christianity is a pedagogy of freedom, it is not just because it leads to freedom, but because its very method of communication activates the freedom of the learner. Kierkegaard insisted that the means used must coincide with the end to be achieved. Since his chief aim was to cultivate 'the individual' his technique must itself create a space in which individuality can be responsibly exercised. He did not want to offer pre-packaged 'answers' nor to acquire disciples and so he actively tried to prevent his own point of view from being straightforwardly and uncritically appropriated by others. What he wanted, as a writer, was to challenge and provoke his readers into thinking and deciding for themselves about the issues he raised. The content of the teaching was itself the actualization of the learner's freedom. In this respect he liked to compare his task with that of Socrates, who, in his own words, had been a kind of midwife, bringing others' thoughts to birth, or, still more apt in Kierkegaard's case, a gadfly, stinging them into thinking for themselves.

Socrates pursued his goal by means of question-and-answer in situations of live dialogue. Kierkegaard, as a writer, had to use different methods, and he developed a range of literary 'alienation effects' to disrupt the sort of immediate sympathy and familiarity which most authors are at pains to establish with their readers. These effects included a baffling variety of pseudonyms, the prolific use of books-within-books, the juxtaposition of diverse literary genres within a single text (e.g., novels, letters, aphorisms, philosophical discourses and sermons all packed together into one book) and other even more complicated and recherché techniques. Reading Kierkegaard is thus a demanding task – even for those who come to it with the appropriate philosophical background.

But if the psychological and literary complexities of Kierkegaard's *oeuvre* can repel, they can also allure. The psychological drama of his work is akin to that of other nineteenth-century 'greats' such as Dostoevsky, Nietzsche, Ibsen and Strindberg and serves, with them, to illuminate the shadow-side of modernity. Similarly, the sheer virtuosity of Kierkegaard's experiments in style, together with his satire, irony and humour, can intrigue readers who might fight shy of any direct Christian apologetic.

It is also worth recalling Kierkegaard's positive contribution to intellectual and cultural history. He is one of the major thinkers of the Christian tradition, and indeed, of Western philosophy as a whole. He is in particular one of the very few Christian thinkers since the Enlightenment to have had any significant impact on secular thought and perhaps the only one to have generated a new secular philosophy, existentialism. We are familiar with Christian theologians adapting or interpreting secular thought for a religious context, but in Kierkegaard's case the relationship is reversed. His achievement here cannot be underestimated – even if there are serious questions to be asked about his particular presentation of Christianity. His work deals with fundamental issues in aesthetics, psychology and cultural history as well as theology and philosophy in the narrow sense, and in all these fields he has made a significant contribution to humanity's self-understanding. Despite the problems posed by his mystifying literary techniques, his work contains many passages of lively and even brilliant prose. Although little of his stylistic virtuosity survives translation, the vividness of his imagery, his mordant aphorisms, delicately drawn parables and cruel satires serve to refresh readers overwhelmed by the intellectual density that characterizes so much of his work, and many artists and writers have had little difficulty in seeing him as one of their own.

Comparing the debit and credit columns, it might be said that Kierkegaard stands before us like a lonely and forbidding mountain in the midst of the cultural landscape, his life and work together confronting us with a colossal question with which we must reckon – even if it is only the more adventurous spirits who will want to try for themselves its icy, jagged peaks. But by what route can we approach this daunting phenomenon, and how can its significance be interpreted to those who do not wish to try for themselves its solitary and dangerous ascents?

In the century and a half since his death, Kierkegaard's work has inspired many different interpretations, each highly revelatory of the interests and viewpoints of the interpreter while none the less giving us something of the impact of Kierkegaard's many-aspected thought. For Henrik Ibsen he was the prototype of the 'enemy of the people', the incorruptibly honest individual who is prepared to stand up, defy, and, if necessary, be broken by the half-truths and double-mindedness of bourgeois conformism. For Karl Barth and the dialectical theologians of post-World War I Germany he was the prophet of the 'infinite qualitative difference' between God and man, proclaiming the abyss in which all human culture is brought to nothing before the transcendent majesty of God. For Heidegger and Sartre he was the first to describe the anguish of the individual who struggles to assert their primordial freedom in an indifferent and impersonal world. For Thomas Mann he was one who saw into the demonic aspects of the artistic vocation, for Malcolm Muggeridge the great debunker of the mass media of modern society and for Mark C. Taylor a precursor of postmodernism – and so the list goes on. All of these represent a partial answer to the question as to what 'Kierkegaard', man, thinker, writer, means, and I cannot hope to offer more than just such a partial answer here, since my own intellectual portrait of him will inevitably be shaped by the particular questions and concerns that shape my own interpretative horizon. None the less, it is possible to sketch in something of that horizon and so offer some level of control in relation to the principle of hermeneutic uncertainty. What then is the question, what is the context, and what is the viewpoint from which this present study is undertaken?

I believe that one of the best points of contact between Kierkegaard and our contemporary situation is to be found in the crisis of faith, which, as I hope to show, is considerably more than a merely 'religious' crisis, of interest only to members of religious communities. What, then, is meant by 'the crisis of faith'? A preliminary answer to this question can be found by looking at the way in which the whole issue of doubt regarding the metaphysical and scriptural bases of the Christian world-view has over the last few years been brought out of the closet of academic theology into the arena of public debate through a series of books, television programmes and episcopal statements of a revisionist persuasion. What is especially remarkable about this recent debate is the way in which it aroused the interest of a supposedly secularized public. It was able to do this because it touched on fundamental matters of authority and doubt, meaning and purpose which are of concern to humanists and secularists as much as to Christians and other religious believers. Perhaps it is a sign that the crisis of meaninglessness, as Tillich called it, is now beginning to disturb the complacency of the

Anglo-Saxon outlook across a whole range of social and intellectual questions. For it is clear that the logical positivist approach to philosophy is losing its stranglehold on British philosophy and is, for whatever reasons, increasingly incapable of addressing the questions with which the post-1960s generations are concerned. In a world which is increasingly disturbed and disturbing, the dry 'common sense' of the traditional so-called 'Oxford' philosophers appears to many as a prime example of academic sterility, nor does this philosophy's concern with 'ordinary language' help it to speak to an age whose skies are tinged with the lurid colours of nuclear and environmental apocalypse. For the present crisis is much more than a crisis in the theoretical fields of theology and philosophy. It is a crisis which manifests itself in many areas of social and political life and its roots thrust beyond intellectual speculation and questioning into the dynamics of modern technology, dynamics that not only overturn established patterns of industrial and social life, but also create new moral dilemmas. Contraception, genetic engineering, medical technology, nuclear energy and nuclear weapons are among the phenomena which indicate the presence of a new and as yet uncharted world in which the old institutions and the old values are unable to provide the customary assurance that all shall be well. During the Cold War era, the most powerful symbol of this crisis was the ever-present possibility of a catastrophic nuclear exchange. Yet if World War III is no longer such an immediately powerful symbol of the ambivalence of scientific progress, the underlying issue continues to press in on us in many ways.

For the awesome powers with which science has equipped us have put into question humanity's total relation to its own history and to its natural environment. It is this totalization of the question of human existence which makes the issues raised by, for example, David Jenkins and Don Cupitt of more than merely theological concern. We are now confronted with the spectre long since predicted by Friedrich Nietzsche: the spectre of an absolute nihilism for which no form of life, no institution, no fact, no value is immune from corrosive scepticism. Nietzsche defined nihilism as the situation in which 'the highest values devaluate themselves. The aim is lacking; "why"? finds no answer.'[7] Life no longer possesses a fundamental '*raison d'être*'.

This crisis does not just concern humanity's view of the extra-human world, but cuts in to the understanding of human existence itself. Humanity itself has become a questionable being, a being without substance, a chain of accidental events without beginning or end. As Rudolf Bultmann put it:

The belief in an eternal order, ruling the life of men, broke down, and with it the ideas of absolute goodness and absolute truth. All this is handed over to the historical process which for its part is understood as a natural process ruled not by spiritual, but by economic, laws. Man is only a process without 'true existence'. The end, it seems, is *nihilism*.[8]

The questioning of the traditional 'realist' view of God leads to the questioning of human being. After the 'death of God' comes the 'death of man'. This situation affects idealistic humanism and dogmatic materialism as much as it does religious belief. For, as Nietzsche already observed, nihilism does not just involve the death of God in the form of a supernatural heavenly Father, but confronts us with the realization that all conceptions of there being an objective aim, unity and purpose to the world originate with us, with the human consciousness of the world, and that the time has now come for us to withdraw these projected structures of meaning and accept the random, purposeless and pluralistic flux of the universe. This Nietzschean challenge is as disturbing to the atheistic or agnostic theories of history propounded by Marxism or Western secularist ideology as it is to a religious view of life, for it unsettles any conviction concerning an overriding, universal structure of meaning to human or cosmic life. When, for instance, an American astronaut speaks of it being 'Man's' destiny to conquer the stars, we have to ask 'Why? Who told us that? Where is it written? Who or what is the source of this "destiny"?' And such questions cannot be answered. We may choose to make it our aim to conquer the stars, but the universe itself is ultimately indifferent to this aim, whether it succeeds or fails. To speak of there being a preordained destiny coming from somewhere 'out there' is simply a way of evading the awesome burden of our own responsibility for the values and aims by which we live. A similar criticism can be made of any theory which presupposes some kind of necessity in history. When the crisis of faith raises fundamental questions as to how we can even begin talking about value, meaning and purpose then theology finds itself on common ground with all who have experienced the sting of modern scepticism and there is a unique opportunity to produce a theological interpretation which not only speaks to but speaks with and from the situation of the secular world itself. It is in this wider context that the theological debate about the meaning of 'God' is to be understood and it is at this point that our engagement with Kierkegaard can most fruitfully begin.

It would seem that if Nietzsche's analysis of the situation is at all valid then any talk of God can only be justified with regard to its psychological or subjective impact on the life of the believer. That was certainly how the psychologist C. G. Jung saw it. Jung, like Freud, was considerably influenced by Nietzsche, but whereas Freud regarded all talk of God as an anachronistic and even a psychologically dangerous illusion, Jung felt that religious belief could play a positive role in psychic life. None the less, his view of the scope of belief was very much governed by Nietzsche's strictures.

I put the word 'God' in quotes in order to indicate that we are dealing with an anthropomorphic idea whose dynamism and symbolism are filtered through the medium of the unconscious psyche. Anyone who wants to can at least draw near to the source of such experiences, no matter whether he believes in God or not ... But it will always remain doubtful whether what metaphysics and theology call God and the gods is the real ground of these experiences.[9]

'God', in this perspective, is to be evaluated not in terms of his existence but in terms of his significance in the religious life of the believer – and if, paradoxically, the exigencies of the religious life compel the believer to insist on the actual objective existence of God, then that is not to be taken as any kind of proof for God's existence, but is itself just one aspect of the psychological state of being religious. But can the believer operate within the confines of such a psychological or subjective view of religion? Must he or she not always be compelled to think and speak of and pray to God as to an 'other'? Does the God-relationship not inevitably involve a dimension of what Martin Buber called 'unincludable otherness'? Is it possible in any way to unite the subjective interpretation of religion – the only interpretation open to those who have passed through the fire of Nietzschean nihilism – with the 'other-centredness' required by the religious life itself?

One of the most interesting recent theological attempts to sketch a spirituality without God is to be found in the work of Don Cupitt. Cupitt demands a Nietzschean honesty in facing up to what he sees as the inevitable fact that we can no longer speak of God as substantially existing in anything like the scientific or objective sense of the term.

Many people claim that God acts. But talk of God and God's action belongs only within the context of religious language and imagery. Nowadays not even the most conservative believers can claim to be able to deploy the idea of divine action effectively in the fields of natural and social science, politics and economics.[10]

The believer's experience of God as 'other' can no longer be regarded as conclusive for what is actually the case. Such experience actually goes against the grain of the deepest tendencies of the modern autonomous spirit. For the truly post-Nietzschean believer God can only be defined as 'the central unifying symbol of the religious life'.[11] In a spirituality appropriate to the modern outlook 'God and the human individual are no longer to be thought of as two beings in opposition ... I and thou are no longer numerically two, but a kind of resonating one.'[12] On this account, as Cupitt himself claims, 'the gap between [Buddhism] and theism is largely closed'.[13]

This crisis in the experience and concept of God takes us to the heart of Kierkegaard's authorship, for what we see here is a monumental attempt to hold together the believer's insistence on the otherness and real transcendence of God and the recognition – a recognition which Kierkegaard also regards as intrinsic to the religious life itself and not just a kowtowing to secular trends – that subjectivity is the proper medium of the religious life. What he effectively tries to do is to draw the total content of traditional faith into the field of subjectivity, yet without reducing it to subjectivism or embracing the reductionist strategy of a Feuerbach (and, some might say, a Cupitt). This not only involves him in a debate with theological defenders of the objectivity of Christian belief over against modern critics of religion, but also leads to a critique of those structures of modern life and thought which assert the primacy of the objective world (whether that is conceived of metaphysically or historically) and thereby inhibit the development of the subjective spirit which is the essential presupposition of faith.

Much of this is relevant to the 'discovery' of Kierkegaard by those involved with the 'dialectical theology' that came to prominence in the German-speaking world in the years following World War I. One of the great emphases of this movement was on the nullity of all human culture and the absolute transcendence of God. In Karl Barth's epochal commentary on Paul's letter to the Romans, Kierkegaard was hailed as the prophet who announced the 'infinite qualitative distinction' between God and 'Man', the one who insisted on the absolute priority of God in the religious life and the irrelevance (or worse) of any so-called theology basing itself on human reason. There is no doubt that this interpretation truly reflects one aspect of Kierkegaard's religious thought which is thoroughly imbued with a sense of the transcendent majesty of God. The religious life, for him, is altogether and utterly God-centred and requires a complete and undivided devotion to God's will.

> It is required of man ... that he shall lose himself in God. If he does this with all his heart, with all his might, and with all his soul then he is in a happy relation to God as the Mighty One, then he worships ... It is now the worshipper's only wish to grow weaker and weaker, for then so much the more worship; it is worship's only need that God grows mightier and mightier. The worshipper is weak ... he is completely weak; he is not able like other people to make decisions for a long life, no, he is completely weak; he is scarcely able to make decisions for the morrow without adding 'If God wills it'. (CD, pp. 136–7)

The annihilation of the human element in the religious relationship is carried to almost morbid extremes in some passages, which I shall examine in a later chapter (see chapter 7, below). For the time being it is sufficient simply to note the strong presence of other-directedness in Kierkegaard's conception of religion. But the way in which he presents this otherness is quite different from the approach of fundamentalistic literalism. The debate between fundamentalism and historical criticism as to what actually happened or what is actually the case is irrelevant to the project of faith, as he sees it. The truth of Christianity does not consist in historically verifiable facts nor in philosophically demon-strable truths but is rooted and grounded in the subjective passion of the individual believer in such a way that the more we are able to enter into our own subjectivity the more we are able to believe. Subjectivity *is* truth (cf. CUP I, pp. 189ff.). His first major work, *Either-Or*, concluded by echoing Luther's dictum that Christ is only real when he is real 'for us': 'only the truth which edifies is truth for you' (EO 2, p. 354). Religious truth cannot be separated from the individual's striving to live out the religious life. There can be no true talk of God outside the passion of faith, or, at least, the passion which seeks or is concerned about faith. Even the otherness, the majesty and the pre-eminence of God can only be spoken of in this context of subjectivity. Kierkegaard is fully prepared to stretch this tension to the limits of paradox.

> In fables and fairy-tales there is a lamp, which is called 'magical'; when it is rubbed, then the spirit (of the lamp) appears. An amusement. But freedom, it is the (true) magic lamp; when a

person rubs it with ethical passion: then God comes into existence for him. And behold, the spirit of the lamp is a servant ... but he who rubs the magic lamp of freedom, he becomes a servant – the Spirit is Lord. This is the beginning. (CUP I, pp. 138–9)

Here the tension between the spirit of autonomous freedom and the religious claim concerning the otherness and Lordship of God is brought to breaking-point. Neither pole can be removed without destroying the truth of the other. It is only in the light of the subjective activation of freedom that 'God comes into existence' – and yet it is only in recognizing God as Lord and ourselves as servants that we express the truth of the relationship which freedom itself has brought about. Cupitt, then, would seem to be in accord with Kierkegaard in declaring that 'religion forbids that there should be any extra-religious reality of God'.[14] And yet Kierkegaard also seems to be saying that 'taking leave of God' as a scientific, philosophical or historical truth by no means requires the reduction of God to a 'resonating one'.

Is Kierkegaard's balancing act successful in the context of his own life and authorship? And, if not, is this because it is intrinsically incoherent or because of certain peculiarities in his highly idiosyncratic approach? These questions will continue to haunt this exploration of Kierkegaard's work as we try to see what subjective faith meant to him. However, as has already been noted, his method is typically indirect, working from the internal critique of false views on truth towards an existential confrontation with the spirit of subjectivity. The method of this study will therefore follow a similar negative path, tracking Kierkegaard's critique of what he regarded as the dominant modes of objectified existence which inhibit the emergence of authentic freedom and therefore also prevent genuine talk of God from taking place. Above all, I shall try to suggest that he saw the struggle between objectivity and faith as very much a problem of the modern world, shaped by a very specific historical and cultural configuration of events and the interpretations of those events. I suggest that even if Kierkegaard's account of faith does turn out to be flawed (as, perhaps, all accounts of faith must be), his posing of the question retains something of its urgency and freshness, since the religious crisis which he pinpoints, a crisis also illuminated by Nietzsche's account of nihilism, is still very much with us, perhaps more than ever before. I shall therefore begin by looking at his interpretation of the present age as an age of systematic and institutionalized unbelief.

TWO

CRITIQUE OF THE AGE

———

ALTHOUGH KIERKEGAARD'S CAREER could easily be represented as a series of polemical outbursts against a succession of intellectual 'foes' (many of whom are, at least outside Denmark, only remembered as the objects of one or another of his attacks), he saw quite clearly that the dulling of the religiously vital sense of subjectivity could not be blamed merely on the unbelief or inappropriately formulated beliefs of a few theologians and philosophers. It was not just one or two thinkers who were in error – the age itself was sick. The crisis of faith was not just an intellectual crisis but involved complex connections between science, technology, social change and religion: in short it concerned the whole of what we have come to call 'modernity'. Although the level and pace of social and technical change was much lower in Kierkegaard's Denmark than in many other countries before or since, and although Denmark was spared many of the severe traumas of industrialization which, for example, scarred the history of early nineteenth-century Britain, there was sufficient ferment in the Danish situation to provide a powerful stimulus to reflection on the forces which lay behind these changes. Kierkegaard's own father had been born a bondsman, and had had to purchase his freedom from indentured service, while the son lived to see, albeit reluctantly, the demise of Danish feudalism and the advent of a democratically controlled constitutional monarchy in a society in which the steam-engine and the telegraph set the agenda for change. Kierkegaard was, of course, by no means the first thinker to direct his attention to the phenomenon of modernism, and before looking at his own account of what he called 'the present age' it is perhaps worthwhile to survey briefly some of his predecessors in this field.

The German poet Friedrich Schiller was one of the pioneers of the line of social criticism, or *Zeitkritik*, which influenced Kierkegaard's development. Schiller's disappointment in the course of the French Revolution, as the dawn of Reason gave way to the bloody zenith of the Terror, provoked him into writing a series of *Letters on the Aesthetic Education of Man*. Although inspired by immediate political events, these *Letters* delved into the forces which this political crisis revealed, above all into the split which the development of reason had brought into human life. 'It was civilization itself which inflicted this wound upon modern man,' he wrote.

> Once the increase of empirical knowledge, and more exact modes of thought, made sharper divisions between the sciences inevitable, and once the increasingly complex machinery of State necessitated a more rigorous separation of ranks and occupations, then the inner unity of human nature was severed too, and a disastrous conflict set its harmonious powers at variance. The intuitive and speculative understanding now withdrew in hostility to take up positions in their respective fields ... While in the one a riotous imagination ravages the hard-won fruits of the intellect, in another the spirit of abstraction stifles the fire at which the heart should have warmed itself and the imagination been kindled.[1]

After Schiller, the problem of how to restore the lost 'inner unity of human nature' became a recurrent motif in German literature and philosophy. Romanticism and Hegelianism each attempted to articulate a reconciliation of the divided self of humanity. Whereas, however, the former turned to aesthetic experience as the focus of a new 'coincidence of opposites', the latter attempted to establish a logical interpretation of history which would explain us to ourselves and justify the dissonances of history as the necessary pre-conditions of a final harmony. In the event, neither of these attempts to restore the shattered edifice of the renaissance ideal proved satisfactory, and with each decade that passed the crisis seemed to grow both in intensity and scope. Faith in an eternal and inviolable natural and human order became ever harder to sustain. Over against the immense optimism of the Hegelian synthesis of the rational and the real a number of less eirenic voices began to be heard. For Feuerbach and Marx it was the historical, this-worldly development of humanity's materialistically conceived 'species-being' which constituted the sole viable goal of human striving. For Marx this meant the intensification, not the healing, of the divisions within society: harmony could only be won by revolutionary conflict. At another intellectual extreme, Arthur Schopenhauer saw the world as the product of a blind urge or will to life. But Schopenhauer did not share the left's aspiration to make the most of humanity's materiality. Instead he sought the final extinction of the self, its complete dissociation from the whole realm of phenomenal reality with its attendant agonies and conflict. Bourgeois conformism rejected both of these 'solutions' to the human predicament, but its coupling of practical materialism to a religious or vaguely idealistic value-system could secure only a fragile peace and, in effect, renounced any attempt to understand or to control the social, scientific and technical processes which the Enlightenment had set in motion. For the young intellectuals of Kierkegaard's day the ideal of harmony, of the reconciliation of the ideal and the real, of reason and sense, was almost impossible to take seriously, and many abandoned themselves to one or other form of pessimism.

Of the figures of the preceding generation it was perhaps the poet and philosopher Poul Martin Møller who stood closest to Kierkegaard, who admired Møller as a teacher and treasured him as a friend. Little known outside Scandinavia, Møller had led an adventurous youth, travelling as a ship's chaplain to China, and returning to meet with some success as a poet before teaching philosophy in Norway and, later, Copenhagen, where he met and befriended Kierkegaard, at that time still a student. Møller was by nature inclined to the ideals of those like Schiller who sought to reunify the divided self of modern humanity. None the less he was led by a long study of modern thought, especially Schopenhauer, to the conclusion that these ideals could not be fulfilled in practice. Modern philosophy, including Hegelianism, had, he believed, no place for the concept of a fully rounded personality. The harmonious aesthetic and religious culture for which he longed, was, he came to realize, a distant, if not an impossible, dream. He felt that the anti-personal forces operative in the present were likely to grow rather than to diminish in power. 'It is possible', he wrote,

> that nihilism has still not reached the point which must be reached so that it can be made apparent that the desolation it brings with it is not the sphere in which the human spirit is at home ... Those who do not share the peculiar passion for destruction may nevertheless seek to build themselves an ark in which they can establish themselves in the hope of better times.[2]

He also expressed his attitude towards nihilism in verse:

> In melancholy hours I often bewail
> You, you nineteenth-century rational man.
> Poetry's flower has withered in your fields,
> You seek the promised land in a wilderness.[3]

The human race had, he thought, a long way still to go through this wilderness: indeed the 'nineteenth-century rational man' was still a long way from realizing that the world he was creating was a religious, moral and social wasteland. Møller would doubtless have found much in the history of Europe in the twentieth century to confirm his prognosis.

Kierkegaard shared much of Møller's grave mistrust of the whole modern development, and he took further the view that nineteenth-century 'man' was essentially 'man in revolt'. Although this was most obviously applicable in the case of the revolutionary left, Kierkegaard saw bourgeois conformism in the same terms. This emerges with particular clarity in his attack on the religious self-justification of the bourgeoisie.

Bourgeois religiosity, he declares, is a religion of the lips and not the heart. 'The bourgeois' love of God commences when the vegetative life is in full swing, when the hands are comfortably folded over the stomach, when the head is reclining on a soft, easy chair, and when a drowsy glance is raised toward the ceiling, toward higher things' (JP 220). This practical marginalizing of God and of the ethical claims of religion was, he believed, as much *lèse-majesté* towards God as the avowed atheism of militant communism. The bourgeois social order is itself revolutionary, he argues, although only in a surreptitious and cowardly manner. It does not openly attack existing institutions such as the Church or the monarchy, but undermines the principles of authority and faith for which these institutions originally stood while preserving what becomes a mere façade – it 'lets everything remain standing but cunningly steals away its meaning' (TA, p. 77). This whole bourgeois social order is directed to man's material comfort; the bourgeois virtues of family life, industry and civic duty are all harnessed to the end of making the human race more at home in the world. Bourgeois religion, philosophy and morality are all similarly characterized by the same quality of worldliness.

Kierkegaard pictured one of his fictional pseudonyms, Johannes Climacus, sitting in one of the great public gardens of Copenhagen, smoking a leisurely cigar as he surveys the bustle of activity going on all around him.

'You are getting on', I said to myself, 'and are becoming an old man, without being anything and without really doing anything. Everywhere however, where you look around in literature or in life, you see the renowned names and figures, the valued and acclaimed men

who are stepping forward or being talked about, the many benefactors of the age, who know how to benefit mankind by making life
easier and easier, some by railways, others by omnibuses and
steamships, others by the telegraph, others by easily understood
surveys and brief summaries of everything worth knowing, and
finally the true benefactors of the age, who by the power of thought,
make the life of the spirit easier and easier, yet more and more
important.' (CUP I, p. 186)

One might, of course, ask what is wrong with making life easier and
easier? Must the world continue to be a vale of tears simply because
earlier generations lacked the means to shape their circumstances to
human ends? Isn't Kierkegaard here revealing the kind of spiritual
masochism which has become the hallmark of cultural Jeremiahs of all
kinds? What is wrong, he could retort to such accusations, is that this
comfortable bourgeois world makes itself at home in the world only by
ignoring or even obliterating certain vital qualitative distinctions which
give human life its specific value and dignity, distinctions such as those
between rulers and subjects, between the sexes, between more and less
gifted individuals, and, above all, between the divine and the human.
The price of bourgeois comfortableness is what Kierkegaard calls
'levelling'. Levelling is a process which not only levels off the distinctions between ranks and offices within society but also affects man's
capacity for authentic subjectivity. Real passionate selfhood, Kierkegaard believes, depends on tensions engendered by dynamic contradictions and oppositions within experience – the sort of tensions which
inspire tragic conflict and make demands on human greatness. In the
world produced by levelling, however, all the vital contradictions are
ironed out and life becomes 'one-dimensional'. Humanity loses what
Kierkegaard calls its primitivity.

> ... knowledge more and more turns away from existence's primitive
> impressions: there is nothing to experience, nothing to happen,
> everything is finished and the task of speculation is (simply) to
> find headings for the particular concepts, to classify and method-
> ically arrange them; one does not love, does not believe, does not act,
> but one knows what love, what belief are, and the question is simply
> what their place in the system is ... (CUP I, p. 344)

Kierkegaard fears the advent of a world in which there will be a
terrifying surplus of theory over practice, in which more energy will be

spent on understanding life than living it, and in which the institution-alized organization of ways of satisfying human needs will drown out the real subjective sense of what is actually needful as life is reduced to a 'shadow existence' (CUP I, p. 344). It must be said again that this is not just the fault of speculative philosophers but inheres in the very structures of modern urban society. 'In the great cities of the modern world people are too crowded together, too protected to experience their own primitivity. To know that, one must be able to hear the call of the wild, the cry of the wolf and know what it is to be afraid' (cf. SLW, pp. 379–80).

In addition to the emotional impoverishment it engenders, a key feature of this loss of primitivity is the drying-up of the springs of action.

> The present age is essentially the rational, reflecting, *unimpassioned age, briefly flaring up with enthusiasm and cunningly relaxing in indolence.* If one ... had figures for the consumption of rationality from generation to generation one would be astonished to see what a monstrous quantity was being consumed today ... I wonder if there is one person left who just once commits a colossal blunder? Even a suicide today scarcely ever kills himself from desperation, but considers the act for so long and so rationally, that he is throttled by rationality ... In contrast to the age of revolution which was an age of action, the present age is the age of publicity ... Action and decision are as little to be found in the present age as the joy of swimming dangerously is to be found among those who swim in the shallows. (TA, pp. 68–71)

This kind of analysis of modernity, an analysis which characterizes industrial civilization as essentially rationalizing and voyeuristic rather than instinctive and active, remains very influential. Jung, for instance, wrote that 'As scientific understanding has grown, so our world has become dehumanized. Man feels himself isolated in the cosmos, because he is no longer involved in nature ... the surface of our world seems to be cleansed of all superstitious and irrational elements.'[4] The human consequences of this situation are spelled out by one of Jung's closest collaborators, M.-L. von Franz:

> Nowadays more and more people, especially those who live in large cities, suffer from a terrible emptiness and boredom, as if they were waiting for something that never arrives. Movies and television,

spectator sports and political excitements may divert them for a while, but again and again, exhausted and disenchanted, they have to return to the waste-land of their own lives.[5]

This is akin to Kierkegaard's complaint regarding the ease and superficiality of modern life. It could be dismissed as mere nostalgia for an imaginary heroic past that probably never existed. Even so, it reflects a widely held view that technological progress cannot of itself solve all the problems of humanity and that the critique of progress is also humanistic, a point that has been recognized by Jules Henry, who wrote of Kierkegaard's critique of the age that 'This is humanism: perhaps humanism's most eloquent defender against the march of the science that men feel threatening them. In this context, perhaps, primitiveness becomes humanism.'[6]

What Kierkegaard calls 'reflection' plays a major part in the process by which the capacity for primitiveness is destroyed. He takes this term from Hegelianism and uses it in a precise technical sense. Reflection is conceived as a function of mind, manifesting itself both in the individual and the social life, in which a sharp distinction is drawn between subject and object. For instance, in the sphere of knowledge reflection means that way of knowing in which the object is not apprehended in immediate intuition but is known as it is reflected in the consciousness of the knowing subject. There is no confusion, no identity, of subject and object. Reflection is therefore fundamentally dualistic and can be used to denote those situations in which feeling is separated from thought, religion from science and the individual from society.

In its positive aspect reflection reveals humanity's ability to step back from the continuum of natural being and (in Bacon's phrase) to put nature on the rack, to ask questions and to develop a many-faceted cultural existence, free from the immediate pressures of animal survival. Through the philosophy of Descartes, reflection, in the form of methodical doubt, comes to be embodied in the basic outlook of the scientific era. Without reflection no science, no technology, no 'Enlightenment' (in the sense of the eighteenth century) would be possible. But Enlightenment culture also involves the separation from and rooting out of previous forms of culture and life. Kierkegaard saw the Christian desecration of the sacred woods of the ancient Teutonic world as a paradigmatic example of the *modus operandi* of such 'Enlightenment' and of the spirit of reflection by which it is shaped (EPW, p. 64). Radical reflection involves the refusal to accept any pre-existent values and taboos and the challenging of whatever is merely 'given', whether in society or in humanity's relation to the natural world. Ultimately it evolves into an all-embracing attack upon the established order, whether this attack is overt, as in the case of communism, or covert, as in the case of the bourgeois revolution. But this attack on what is given brings about a diminution of reality. Man masters the world in which he finds himself – but in mastering it loses touch with it, and, implicitly, loses touch with himself. For we do not create ourselves, and a quality of givenness belongs to our essential being. Reflection obscures this primordial dependence and thus alienates us from our own nature.

The Catholic theologian Walter Kasper succinctly describes this situation in commenting on Hegel's early writings:

> The emancipation in modern times of the [human] subject reduced the external world increasingly to the status of mere object: the dead material for man's ever more unrelenting domination of the world, a domination achieved with the aid of modern science and technology. External reality was increasingly demythologized and desacralized. Religion however withdrew more and more into the individual; it became a character-less, empty longing for the infinite ... Ultimately, however, there is a yawning gulf on both sides – the objective and the subjective. The outer world turns neutral and banal; the inner world of the individual becomes hollow and empty.[7]

The empty subjectivity of reflection thus paradoxically serves to bring about a constant objectification of the world, an objectification embodied in scientific knowledge and in social organization. Although Hegel himself was aware of this dialectic, Kierkegaard sees Hegel's own philosophical system as an outstanding theoretical expression of the tendency to objectification. Karl Marx saw a similar tendency in Hegelianism, but whereas he was concerned about the way in which this objectification involved the subordination of the humanity of the industrial worker to the realm of commodity-objects which the worker's whole existence was geared to producing, Kierkegaard was more concerned with the way in which religion, dependent as it is on the passionate subjectivity of the individual, was distortingly objectified in state-controlled institutions, in doctrinal systems of theology and in speculative philosophy. This objectification worked against the element of personal decision which he regarded as necessary to authentic faith. 'Faith does not result from straightforward scientific considerations ... on the contrary, in this objectivity one loses that infinite personal interestedness in passion which is the condition of faith ...' (CUP 1, p. 29). It is not only the Hegelians and other critics of traditional faith who are guilty of this objectifying approach, however, but the orthodox and the Revivalists commit the same error. They see the dispute about Christianity as being a dispute about facts. No, says Kierkegaard, this is not it at all. Facts belong to the dimension of reflection on life. The issue has to be relocated in the irreducibly individual and primitive starting-point of all knowledge and experience.

The tendency to objectification makes itself present in the way in which modern humanity avoids responsibility by trying to see life from a world-historical perspective.

> The more the collective idea takes the leading role even at the popular level, the more fearful it becomes to make the transition from identifying oneself with the race and saying, 'We, our age, the nineteenth century' to becoming an individual existing human being ... In the midst of all the jubilation over 'our age' and 'the nineteenth century' there is a hidden note of concealed contempt for humanity; in the midst of the generation's (self-)importance there is a despair about what it is to be human. All, all want to join in, everyone wants to fall under the spell of the totality, 'world-historically', no one wants to be an individual existing human being. (CUP 1, pp. 354–5)

In this connection Kierkegaard is as contemptuous of the world-historical perspectives of the Nordic nationalist followers of N. F. S. Gruntvig as he is of the Hegelians. None the less Hegelianism more **than** any other philosophy gave the objectifying, world-historical approach a systematically coherent form by attempting to establish a universal network of dialectical laws governing the form of every phenomenon in the natural as well as in the human world. Hegelianism responded to the 'need' of the individual to justify himself by virtue of his place in a total scheme of things, and believed that this accorded with the 'systematic' character of the age, which, according to one of the contemporary Danish Hegelians,

> ... is the period of the system, not only in the more narrow philosophical and scientific sense, but in respect of religious, poetical, yes, even industrial and mercantile systems. The *universal* has become an acknowledged power over against which every particular interest steps back.[8]

Kierkegaard for his part objected that the 'universality' of the system was a false universality, gained at the price of simply leaving out whatever aspects of the real world refused to fit in to the systematic blueprint. Blinded by the system (including 'the industrial and mercantile systems' of the bourgeois world), humanity loses touch with its telluric, earthly being – the only place the system could be perfectly realized, Kierkegaard wryly comments, would be on the moon (CUP I, p. 124).

A basic feature of the systematic view of life is the belief that all facts and all values can be slotted without exception into a common frame of reference. This belief implicitly rejects any notion of either things or people possessing a quality of irreducible uniqueness. In philosophy this is reflected in the Hegelian idea that every concept can be mediated by or correlated with the other concepts of the systematic whole; in the market-place it means that every thing and every man has its price. The philosophical system reflects a society in which exchangeability has been made the principle governing all relationships.

In a later chapter we shall pursue Kierkegaard's more narrowly philosophical objections to the Hegelian system. What needs to be noted here is the cultural dimension of his critique. For he argues that the systematic principle of universal exchangeability reflects a basic attitude which can be described as 'comparison', 'envy' or 'fear'. This in turn can be seen as a manifestation of the predominance of reflection in that reflection has broken the natural bonds of basic trust within society, and the universal desire to have what the others have, to be like the others, is an attempt to compensate for this loss. 'Modern man' (and perhaps the gender-specific term is appropriate here: it certainly reflects much of the spirit of nineteenth-century progressive humanism) is fated to seek (fruitlessly) in and through others the divine image of humanity which he neglects to find in himself, condemned to want 'this man's gift and that man's scope'. He forgets the sheer intrinsic glory of being human which belongs to every individual.

> Ah! In comparison's busy and worldly life those great, uplifting, simple first thoughts are more and more forgotten, perhaps completely. One man compares himself with another, one generation compares itself with another – and so the mass of comparisons grows and piles up over mankind's head. (UDVS, p. 189)

This state of incessantly comparing oneself with others can be described in more moral terms as 'envy' or 'fear'. However, Kierkegaard claims that he does not use envy in this sense moralistically, but as a way of spelling out 'reflection's idea'. It is an attitude implied in the social divisions, the separation of individuals from one another, brought about by reflection, and reveals the profound insecurity which the modern situation engenders.

> Gradually, as a certain superficial culture spreads itself, and with it the various relationships which link people to one another are multiplied, gradually as constant comparison's envious and fearful pettiness spreads its infection, it is unfortunately as if everything is aiming at quelling humanity's courage. At the same time as struggles are undertaken to overthrow authorities and governments people seem as if they are working towards producing the most dangerous thraldom of all: man's petty-minded fear of his equal. (UDVS, p. 328)

Behind the easy and comfortable façade of bourgeois society lurks a quiet despair, a profound failure of the courage to be. This is Kierkegaard's vision of the acquisitive society in which 'having' functions as a feeble substitute for assured and self-confident 'being'. Such envious and fearful comparing of oneself with others is not however confined to the acquiring of material goods. Kierkegaard found many examples of it in daily life, especially at the time when he came under attack from *The Corsair*, a widely circulated satirical newspaper which made him an object of mockery as he went on his daily perambulations through the streets of Copenhagen. In the way he was treated during this persecution, Kierkegaard saw how infinitely malleable people became under the spell of envy.

> ... when I walk into a place where several people have congregated, it often happens that one or the other arms himself against me by laughing; presumably he feels that he is the agent of public opinion. But when I address a word to him, the same man becomes extremely docile and cordial. That is, basically he regards me as somebody important ... but if he cannot manage to participate, as it were, in my greatness, then he laughs at me. As soon as he becomes participant, so to speak, he boasts of my greatness. (JP 6031)

He illustrates the point with an anecdotal account of how one day he became aware of three youths sniggering at him as he walked by. Noticing that they were smoking, he walked over and asked them for a

light – immediately their manner changed and they all doffed their caps
to him!

The desire of acquisitive and envious comparison 'to be like the
others expresses mankind's degeneration, its degradation to copies,
numbers' (JP 2973), and ultimately leads to a regression to the animal
herd-instinct which Kierkegaard regards as the real 'opium of the
people'. He wrote that '... the numerical transfers mankind to an
exalted state just as opium does, and he is so tranquillized by the
trustworthiness of millions' (JP 2980). To identify with the millions, the
majority, to become one of the crowd, is, Kierkegaard believes, the
surest way to defend oneself against the demands of religion and ethics.

> The crowd – not this one or that one, the living one or the dead one,
> the lowly one or the distinguished one, the rich one or the poor one,
> etc., but the crowd understood in its very essence – is untruth, in that
> a crowd either completely renders the individual impenitent or
> irresponsible, or weakens his sense of responsibility by making
> him a part. (PV, p. 114)

The most significant contemporary form of the crowd in modern times
is, in Kierkegaard's view, not a street mob but 'the public', a faceless,
invisible abstraction which is everywhere and nowhere.

> The public is not a people, not a generation, not one's contempor-
> aries, not a community, not a society, not these particular people, for
> all such are only what they are by virtue of their concrete form; not
> one of those who belongs to 'the public' however has any essential
> commitment ... The public is some monstrous Something, the
> abstract wasteland and void which is all and nothing ... it is the
> most dangerous of all powers and the most meaningless ... (TA, pp.
> 92–3)

Kierkegaard was deeply perturbed by the role which he saw 'the public'
coming to play in bourgeois politics. When he speaks of humanity
entering a period which can be characterized as the tyranny of the
masses, of the crowd, he is not thinking of 'the masses' in the Marxist
sense, but of 'the public', which is very much a bourgeois phenomenon.
Politics carried on in the name of the public soon reveals itself to be
another form of the 'deification of statistics', constantly invoking the
aid of opinion polls and the silent majority. The root of it all is, as we
have seen, the basic cowardliness which flies from responsibility and

enviously and fearfully tries to be 'like the others' by thinking as the public, this 'all and nothing', thinks.

The emergence of the modern public is, Kierkegaard suggests, intimately associated with the rise of the press. The press is actually the agent by which power is shifted from its established and previously recognized centres to the public. The press demands total publicity in political affairs, thereby abolishing the notion 'that there are a few individuals who are more insightful than others and for that very reason are able to see so much further than they are able to pilot; but total publicity is grounded on the idea that everybody should govern' (JP 4192). And that, if Kierkegaard is right about the essential nature of the public, means that actually nobody governs, nobody is ultimately answerable. Again it is important to remember that what he actually saw taking shape in his own day was not the rise of one of the great dictatorships which were to frighten whole peoples into conformity in the twentieth century, but the beginnings of a relatively open bourgeois democracy. It is not the dangers of an Orwellian police state he is warning against, but those of democratic conformism.

His attack on the role of the press in all this was merciless, and he could go so far as to label the press 'the evil principle in the modern world' (JP 2148). Doubtless his feelings on this point were affected by the humiliating vilification he suffered at the hands of *The Corsair*, but the influence with which he credited the press went well beyond what he might have inferred from his own experiences. He could even speak of the press as having 'produced' 'the advance of civilization, the rise of the large cities, centralization' (JP 4166). The press, in other words, is not just one manifestation among others of the modern spirit, but belongs to the dynamic base of modern urban and technological society. In the light of the expansion of the means of mass media in the twentieth century and the as yet incalculable significance of the contemporary communications revolution this point is perhaps even more plausible today than it was in Kierkegaard's own time. The rapid communication of highly condensed and well-packaged information is an absolutely indispensable element in the maintenance of modern society, in scientific and intellectual life as well as in business and politics.

Despite the obvious differences between the necessary superficiality of popular journalism and the rigorous abstractions of Hegelian philosophy, Kierkegaard saw both of them as examples of impersonal communication. Authentic language depends on the existence of a responsible subject, but the expansion of the modes of impersonal communication both reflects and heightens a crisis in language itself as words are devalued, stripped of their rich inheritance of associations and reduced to bits of information devoid of ethical significance or to meaningless jargon. In the age of reflection language is reduced to 'idle chatter' (TA, pp. 97ff.). Yet there is a tragic element in this, since the reflective act itself, the separation of subject and object, is an essential presupposition of language. But when reflection goes too far then language is incapable of mirroring the subjective primitivity that characterizes genuinely meaningful speech. Commenting on a contemporary financial crisis, Kierkegaard observed that 'At the moment the greatest fear is of the total bankruptcy toward which all Europe seems to be moving and men forget the far greater danger, a seemingly unavoidable bankruptcy in an intellectual-spiritual sense, a confusion of language ...' (JP 5181). He was no enemy of language, and delighted in his own (albeit erratic) mastery of the Danish mother-tongue, but he returned again and again to the theme that modern man, man whose life is qualified throughout by reflection, talks too much, and that perhaps the most direct way of breaking the grip of reflection would be to become silent. The ability to become silent is a hallmark of authentic religiosity.

It is man's advantage over the animal kingdom that he can talk; but in relation to God this can easily become man's downfall, that he can and wants to talk. God is in heaven, man on earth, therefore they cannot easily talk together. When prayer really becomes prayer, then it becomes silence. (CD, p. 323)

But such a capacity for silence is increasingly alien to modern man – although Kierkegaard seems to think it is not so alien to woman (FSE/ JY, pp. 46–51). The point of such silence – and this applies in the human sphere as well as between the divine and the human – is not to put an end to language, but to create a space in which words can acquire their proper resonance, in which people can not only speak to one another (which they do all too easily anyway) but also *hear* what is being said.

This sense of a crisis in language itself certainly influenced Kierkegaard in his concern to forge an indirect method of communication, a method that would defy all attempts at facile and superficial appropriation and would bring about a pause in the otherwise non-stop flow of verbiage that carries writers and readers alike off into meaninglessness. Without such a method, he believed, his work could too easily turn into a quasi-political cause (perhaps a kind of party of individualism) or else be neatly slotted into the system (as some Kierkegaard interpreters have since managed to do). He recognized that difficult as it is to leave open the circle of discourse, it is only such linguistic openness that allows for the authentic expression of primitive freedom and responsibility. Unless this happens, even the most personal words, words such as 'God' and 'love', become mere ciphers for sentimental and meaningless generalizations. Language loses its subject and we no longer know what it really is to say 'I'. It is to the reawakening of the sense of subjectivity – in language, but also in life as the necessary precondition and ground of language – that Kierkegaard's authorship is directed: against the levelling reflective spirit of the modern age.

These remarks also throw light on Kierkegaard's relation to postmodernity, in so far as exponents of postmodernism embrace the view that, since the very structures of language entail the endless deferring of meaning, language is essentially subject-less. In the climate of postmodernity all claims regarding the possibility of an authentic voice are dismissed as residual idealism (or worse), so that, in this respect at least, Kierkegaard must count as a critic of postmodernity. However, he shares with many postmodernists an understanding of the extremely problematic nature of the quest for such an authentic voice and the virtual impossibility of justifying it on the plane of objective knowledge.

THREE

CRITIQUE OF SOCIETY

———

HOW DID THE spirit of the age manifest itself with regard to the concrete forms of social life, and were the prevailing institutions of society able to withstand the encroachments of levelling? As we look into these questions it soon becomes clear that although Kierkegaard's natural conservatism led him to oppose the main features of modernism and all doctrines of social progress, he did not believe that it would be in any real sense possible to turn the clock back and simply restore the old institutions. For the fact is that these institutions failed to prevent the bourgeois revolution, a revolution that allowed them to retain their outward forms – monarchy, marriage, the established Church – while robbing them of power and meaning. A pattern soon emerges as we look into this part of Kierkegaard's thought: what is legitimate in a context where claims to authority and meaning rest on faith in the divine world-order is radically devalued when, as in the typical modern situation, its legitimacy is seen to depend on the extent to which it can be rationally or functionally justified – or simply the extent to which it is acceptable to 'the public'. For example, when marriage is no longer held to be 'instituted of God himself' and therefore a duty incumbent on all who have no special vocation to the single state, but is instead evaluated in terms of various humanistic criteria (e.g., personal and sexual fulfilment, economic security, etc.), it loses its former absoluteness, so that it can no longer be considered valid if it fails to achieve the goals to which it is now subordinated. The bourgeois claims regarding the sanctity of the monarchy, property, marriage, etc., must therefore be regarded as false since, in the bourgeois period, the foundation on which such claims depend has been removed by the rationalizing, 'enlightening' dynamics of the bourgeois revolution itself. Kierkegaard's conservatism is in a sense so extreme that he is not at all concerned to defend the interests of the actual *status quo* of his day, but rather, as we shall now see in relation to politics, marriage and the Church, to expose their hollowness.

Politics

It will already be clear from the preliminary overview of Kierkegaard's critique of the age that he regarded the development of modern society with grave suspicion. Far from leading to the emancipation of mankind, technology and popular democracy would, he believed, lead to a new tyranny – the tyranny of the masses. With this assumption he looked on contemporary political life as one of the prime focii of the levelling process. By instinct he was one of those conservatives who regard all politics with a certain aloofness, since political activity as such implies a lack of confidence in the way things are. 'No,' he wrote in a letter to a friend, 'politics is not for me' (LD, p. 253). None the less he was throughout his life a keen observer of and commentator on the political situation, both in Denmark itself and, more generally, in Europe, although he avoided being too directly involved in political controversies.

It is therefore somewhat surprising to find that his debut as a writer was in the field of politics, when, as a student, he wrote a series of anti-liberal newspaper articles. In the same period he addressed the University Student Association on the subject 'Our Journalistic Literature', an address which took up some of the themes he had dealt with in the articles. The point at issue was the question of the freedom of the press, and the impact which the July Revolution in France (1830) had on the loosening of press censorship that was prevalent in Denmark during the first third of the nineteenth century, as it was elsewhere. In this debate the young Kierkegaard sought to dispel what he saw as the liberal myth that freedom of the press was being brought about by anti-government agitation. Kierkegaard suggested that in fact the opposite is the case: that it was the government which took the decisive steps, while the liberals merely responded after the event to government action (JP 5116). The details of the debate are of purely historical interest, but in it Kierkegaard is making a serious point of general importance: that the modern desire for emancipation or liberalization is essentially parasitic; far from being the avant-garde of a new order, the vitality of the opposition is the negative vitality which can only thrive by attacking and undermining the substance of the established social order

Kierkegaard used his first book, a lengthy review of Hans Christian Andersen's novel *Only a Fiddler*, to make a similar point. Here he characterizes the activity of the political left as being a translation into the sphere of practice of the same spirit of negation and scepticism which is to be found in Hegelian philosophy. The slogan of this tendency, he says, is

... forget what is actual (and this is already an *attentat*), and, in so far as the forms of state which have been grandly developed over hundreds of years cannot be ignored – then they must be got rid of ... Like Hegel they begin – not the system but – existence with nothing, and the negative moment through which and by the power of which all movement occurs ... is mistrust, which undeniably has such a negative power that – and this is the one good thing about it – it must end by destroying itself. (EPW, p. 64)

This assessment of liberalism is the leitmotif of Kierkegaard's political thought. We can find it again in the correspondence between Kierkegaard and his friend J. L. A. Kolderup-Rosenvinge, a politically conservative professor of law at Copenhagen University. The period of this correspondence, 1847–49, was a tumultuous time in Denmark as elsewhere in Europe. These years saw the setting up of a two-chamber elected assembly with a franchise extended to all male householders over thirty; the abolition of hereditary privileges; the promulgation of freedom of assembly, freedom of speech and freedom of the press; freedom of occupation and universal military conscription. In these two years, then, Denmark moved from an absolute to a constitutional monarchy. Moreover, this same period saw a steady worsening of relations between Denmark and Germany over the question of the German-speaking Danish provinces of Slesvig-Holsten. The liberals played a strongly nationalistic role in this situation, which led in the end to a war that proved disastrous for the Danes and resulted in the eventual handing over of the disputed territories to Prussia. 'As I say', writes Kierkegaard to his friend

... it was a remarkable year, that year of '48. It has, as we have often noted, turned everything upside down ... Suppose a writer were to recreate 'The Catastrophe of '48' in dramatic form ... He would then have to create a wholly new kind of drama, a monstrosity, a drama that makes a mockery of all the rules, a drama in five and a half acts. (LD, p. 300)

Kierkegaard's meaning is that once the revolutionary process has been set in motion there will be no way to stop it, the 'drama' will be incapable of being brought to a conclusion: the measures which the liberals take to 'solve' the crisis, based as they are on the principles of negation and mistrust in the established order, can only ever provide temporary solutions – there will always be an extra half-act left over as the country lurches from crisis to crisis.

In an earlier letter to Kolderup-Rosenvinge, Kierkegaard made great play with a pun on the Danish word 'Bremse', which means both a brake and a gadfly. 'In a newspaper', he tells his friend, 'I had read that on railroad trains something called "a gadfly" is employed – yes, is this not crazy? – to stop' (LD, p. 259). He finds an application of this pun ready to hand in the political situation. 'For', he asks,

> ... is this not the law of confusion that governs recent European events? They wish to stop by means of a revolution and to stop a revolution by means of a counter-revolution. But what is a counter-revolution if it is not also a revolution? And to what can we compare a revolution if not to a gadfly? I am sure you will agree that I am right in considering the whole development in Europe as an enormous scepticism or as a vortex. What does a vortex seek? – A fixed point where it can stop ... For a long time now there has been so much discussion of the need for movement relative to what is established that the need of the established relative to movement has been completely forgotten. (LD, pp. 260–1)

But how can the 'movement', the social and political vortex into which Denmark has fallen, be brought to a halt?

> Most people believe that so long as one has a fixed point *to which* one wants to get, then motion is no vortex. But this a misunderstanding. It all depends on having a fixed point *from which to set out*. Stopping is not possible at a point *ahead*, but at a point *behind* ... Any purely political movement, which accordingly lacks the religious element or is forsaken by God, is a vortex, cannot be stopped, and is prey to the illusion of wanting a fixed point ahead, which is wanting to stop by means of a gadfly; for the fixed point, the only fixed point, lies behind. And therefore my opinion about the whole European confusion is that it cannot be stopped except by religion ... the movement of our time, which appears to be purely political, will turn out to be religious or the need for religion. (LD, p. 262)

Kierkegaard thus takes up a position diametrically opposed to that represented by Ernst Bloch's philosophy of hope. According to Bloch, all religion which understands itself (etymologically correctly) as re-ligio, binding humanity back to its origins, is inherently repressive and anti-humanistic. The God who is 'for' us is the God of the Exodus, the future-directed God whose self-definition is 'I will be what I will be'. He alone is the God who liberates humanity and who functions as a symbolic guarantee of the ultimate fulfilment of man's utopistic aspirations.

Kierkegaard's view, however, is that internal violence and foreign wars are the logical consequence of a political order based on the principle of negation of the established order. 'Schelling is right', he remarks, 'when he says ... "When it comes to the point where the majority decides what constitutes truth, it will not be long before they take to deciding it with their fists"' (JP 4112). And:

> The tragedy at this moment is that the new ministry needs war to survive, needs all the agitation of national feelings possible. Even though we could easily enough have peace – if the ministry is not completely stupid it must see that *it* needs war. (JP 4137)

In the light of these and similar statements we should appreciate that although Kierkegaard's political outlook is indeed permeated by pre-suppositions that are easily portrayed as 'reactionary', his critique of politics is not solely directed against what we would call left-wing or revolutionary movements, but is very much aimed at the sort of political philosophy that might today call itself 'conservative'. His attack on democracy is inextricably intertwined with his attack on nationalism and his denunciation of the propagandist powers of the press. He is not to be written off as a kind of self-appointed Coriolanus, but is in many ways accurately sensitive to the anti-humanistic elements of the emergent bourgeois democracy. If Denmark was spared the worst horrors of industrialization and colonial wars, we should not forget that these too belonged to the 'progress' of the nineteenth century, nor should we forget that the great 'discovery' of Kierkegaard as a thinker coincided with the First World War and the consequent unmasking of many of the ideological self-justifications of Western Europe. Kierkegaard's conservatism enabled him to see the shadow-side of nineteenth-century politics in a way which many liberals could not. Moreover, it is clear that he had no time for Romantic dreams of some counter-revolution to restore the *ancien régime*.

Many of his thoughts on the character and course of modern politics can be found in the review of the novel *Two Ages*, a review he regarded as being in many ways prophetic of the events of 1848. Here he indicates the positive aspect of the levelling process which at first sight he seems to abhor utterly. He explicitly rules out the fantasy that some great leader will appear to guide the nation back to the ways of its forebears. 'The time is now past', he says bluntly (TA, p. 108). Authority can no longer be embodied in tangible, clearly recognizable institutions or figures. The result of levelling will be that each individual must come to make a choice between completely abdicating all personal responsibility to the crowd, 'the public', and a totally individual affirmation of freedom and meaning. Thus it will only be by taking responsibility for their own lives that people will be empowered to transcend the deepening mediocrity of a levelled society.

> And when the generation, which indeed has itself wanted to level, has wanted to be emancipated and to revolt, has wanted to abolish authority and has thereby itself brought about the desolating forest-fire of abstraction by means of the scepticism of association; when this generation has got rid of individualities and all organic concrete forms (again by means of the levelling scepticism of association), when it has instead got 'humanity' and numerical equality between man and man ... then the work begins, then the individuals must help themselves, each on their own. (TA, pp. 107–8)

This 'individualism' should not be interpreted as a call to retreat into the sphere of 'private life' but as an attempt to characterize the sort of equality which Kierkegaard does regard as desirable. The equality which expresses itself in the kind of democratic politics he sees evolving in the present age is, he believes, merely an abstract 'numerical' equality. In real life, he argues, no two people are in any way equal, except in terms of their equal self-responsibility in faith 'before God' and in love to each other.

> There has therefore never lived a man in Christendom, any more than in heathen times, who has not been dressed in or clad with the differences that belong to this earthly life; as little as the Christian lives or can live without a body, just as little can he live without this earthly life's differences, which belong in a particular way to everyone by virtue of birth, class, circumstances, education, etc. – none of us is pure humanity. (WL, p. 70)

The pursuit of abstract equality is, then, the pursuit of a chimera. Christianity is not at all concerned with removing the differences between men in this way, but at the same time, precisely because it does not regard these differences as decisive with regard to what constitutes human worth, it does not value one set of worldly distinctions above another. Both king and beggar are charged by Christianity with the task of 'rising above' their situation in life (WL, p. 72). In faith they are already 'equal'.

> Nevertheless if one is in truth to love one's neighbour, one must remember every moment that the (earthly) difference is a disguise. For ... Christianity has not sought to storm forth to abolish difference, attacking neither distinction nor lowliness ... but it wants these differences to hang loosely on the individual, as loosely as the cloak which the king casts off, in order to show who he is, as loosely as the tattered clothes in which a supernatural being has concealed itself. Now when the difference hangs as loosely as this, then every individual is seen as that essential Other, that which all are equally, in which we are eternally, alike, our likeness. (WL, p. 88)

The political agitation which characterizes the levelling process is concerned to abolish the worldly differences, and betrays the envious desire of the mediocre to get for themselves the advantages of the intellectual and social aristocracy. None the less, when it has removed the distraction of external differences we will be confronted by the task of seeing our neighbour – our divinely equal 'essential other' – in each and every person whom we encounter in a way and to a degree that could not otherwise have come about. Levelling may thus be providentially used to prepare the way for a spirituality of radically interiorized love. Although evil in itself, it may, in Bruce Kirmmse's phrase, serve as a 'saving chastisement'.[1] Levelling opens the way for the emergence of a society in which 'each is responsible for all', a society that will no longer take the form of a faceless mass, an anonymous public. It will be an authentic community.

> The cohesiveness of community comes from each one's being a single individual, and then the idea [i.e., the principle that binds the community together]; the connectedness of a public or rather its disconnectedness consists of the numerical character of everything ..., In community the single individual is a microcosm who qualitatively reproduces the cosmos ... In a public there is no single individual and the whole is nothing ... (JP 2952)

Kierkegaard cannot therefore be said to be seeking a way by which the individual can wash his hands of society: what he is searching for is a form of society based on absolute individual responsibility. It is such a society which the politics of the present age militates against.

Theologically we can illuminate Kierkegaard's writings on politics by reference to the Lutheran doctrine of the two kingdoms. According to this doctrine, the sphere of life regulated by the state is inherently corrupt, and can only be dealt with by the harsh methods of worldly power, symbolized by the sword. None the less, this intrinsically sub-Christian mode of governance is permitted and even ordained by God for the restraint of sin and 'the punishment of wickedness and vice'. It is 'of God' even if it does not directly reveal a Christian character. Kierkegaard – unlike some other modern Lutheran theologians – did not regard this doctrine as a 'timeless truth' but treated it in a fundamentally historical way. He saw that it could not naively be applied to the complexities of modern society since in the present situation the established powers had divested themselves of this divinely ordained authority. The bourgeois revolution had kept the traditional forms of monarchy, Church, judiciary, etc., but had deprived them of their intrinsic content. They were no longer justified by appeal to divine right but by appeal to reason and utility. Thus they were no longer instruments in the hand of God for the administration of society, but tools by which humanity itself sought to mould and direct the social order. The constitutional monarch does not rule by divine permission but by permission of the public. The establishment itself had 'sold out' to rationalism and thereby thrown away its right to unconditional obedience and respect.

Kierkegaard's extreme conservatism could thus lead him to denounce the failings of the establishment as well as of the opposition. This became especially clear in his attack on the Danish state church. Before examining this in more detail, however, we shall turn to the critique of the forms of private life which Kierkegaard saw as characterizing modern society.

Private Life

In an age when many despair of understanding – let alone mastering – the complexities of political life, it is all too common a phenomenon that people retreat from the sphere of social concern into the more comfortable, more manageable world of private life and there to seek, above all in the most intimate of our personal relationships, the meaning which is so elusive in the wider sphere. Kierkegaard discusses this retreat into the private world in terms of his critique of sexuality and of family life. Here too he sees the determining elements of the age of reflection at work, splitting these facets of experience which must be held together if we are to know genuine life-giving relationships.

In the preliminary discussion of problems which a contemporary reader is likely to encounter in studying Kierkegaard it was noted that one of these problems concerns what some might see as his morbid attitude to physicality in general and sexuality in particular. There can be no disguising the fact that, especially in his later writings, Kierkegaard came to regard sexuality as inherently likely to lead humanity away from God and as being 'built entirely on a lie' (JP 3970), not merely with regard to the pleasurableness that has always aroused the suspicions of puritans but even in respect of its basic reproductive function. The lie of sexuality, he believed, is the lie that human life in the world is directed towards happiness, whereas, he maintains (and, he asserts, as early Christianity also taught) reproduction is an act whereby parents drag 'one more immortal soul down into this misery, down into this enormous danger ...' (JP 3970). This rejection of sexuality goes hand in hand with an intense focusing of hope on an eternal blessedness beyond this life, a blessedness which seems to be not so much a resurrection of the flesh as a kind of dis-carnate angelic existence in which all traces of physicality have been sloughed off.

In addition to this 'metaphysical' rejection of sexuality, however, we can also find in Kierkegaard a historically orientated critique of the forms and conditions governing sexuality and family life in the modern age. This historical critique of sexuality is, at least in principle, separable from any metaphysical denial of the body. We shall be looking in a later chapter at the implications of Kierkegaard's other-worldliness for an overall reading of his thought, but here we are simply concerned with his exposure of the falsehoods and self-deceptions which, in bourgeois society, surround this most basic area of human life.

It was above all in Romanticism that Kierkegaard encountered the belief that human fulfilment is to be found in the erotic union of man and woman, in particular in a slim but influential volume by the literary critic Friedrich Schlegel. The book in question was a novel entitled *Lucinde* in which Schlegel celebrated his liaison with Dorothea Veit, daughter of the renowned Jewish philosopher Moses Mendelssohn, and, when the affair began, already a married woman. The concept of love which this novel expressed sees man and woman as respectively embodying the polarities of human existence: spirit and sense, reason and feeling, intellect and emotion, infinity and finitude. Through

'Romantic love' we therefore attain to the reunion of our divided selves, in the complementarity of the male-female relationship. Schlegel toys with the idea of the reversal of sexual roles in which the lovers 'compete with childish pleasure as to who can most deceivingly imitate the other, whether you succeed more in putting on the protective ardour of the man or I in acquiring the attractive submissiveness of the woman'. In this sort of love-play he finds perfectly embodied a wonderful 'allegory of the perfection of male and female into complete humanity'. The lovers have a spontaneous sense of this 'complete humanity', and it is their spontaneous joy in this experience that Schlegel sought to express in the novel.

Kierkegaard regarded Schlegel's thesis with grave suspicion on a number of counts. For a start he doubted Schlegel's claim to naivety and ingenuousness. Far from being the flower of an immediate, passionate love, Kierkegaard sees in *Lucinde* an ironic, highly self-conscious manipulation of people and events. Schlegel, he says, is no Don Juan, but 'a personality who is trapped in reflection' (CI, p. 293). Even in the midst of his enjoyment of Lucinde's love he holds himself aloof – he wants to enjoy but he also wants to experience his enjoyment. He loses himself in love only to the extent that he is enabled to experience the sensation of losing himself.

It is in the figure of the Seducer in *Either-Or* that Kierkegaard gives us his fullest exposition of what Schlegel's concept of love really means. When the mask of spontaneity is stripped away the Seducer is revealed as a cold, cynical figure, trapped in the solitude of his own intellectual egotism. His love-making is never a true falling in love, but is a kind of aesthetic game, carefully constructed to maximize each particular nuance of feeling which the 'chase' evokes. He betrays his ultimate indifference to – and even his contempt for – the women he seduces in a quasi-philosophical discourse on the definition of the feminine, in which he concludes that woman is essentially 'being-for-another'. That is to say, woman has no essential claim to humanity in her own right, but solely through her relation to man: 'that which is for another is not and, as it were, first becomes visible by means of another' (EO 1, p. 431). In volume two of *Either-Or* we are given a thorough analysis of the Seducer's basic life-view in two lengthy letters written to a young aesthete by one 'Assessor William' (or 'Judge William' as some translations refer to him). Over against the irresponsible aesthetic attitude which uses erotic relationships as a means of 'having' certain experiences the Assessor argues for the honouring of marriage as a relationship of mutual openness, a relationship which is not based on the arbitrary whim of the individual, but in the moral and religious law which is concretely embodied in the marriage rites of the Church.

The 1830s had seen a revival of interest in *Lucinde*, when it was hailed as a forerunner of 'the gospel of the emancipation of the flesh' which the materialistic left-wing intelligentsia made one of its rallying-cries. Schleiermacher's defence of the novel was republished with a new introduction that claimed him too as a precursor of such a gospel. It was against this tendency that Kierkegaard's critique of Schlegel was first and foremost directed. However, even though he seems, via the *persona* of Assessor William (a paragon of civic virtue), to be defending 'conventional' marriage against the more 'enlightened' views of the left, his defence is such that it lays the basis for an attack on conventional bourgeois marriage also. The Assessor is, in fact, more than willing to concede a great deal of ground in the face of his young friend's objections to bourgeois marriage. In particular he is highly critical of the attempt to defend marriage by any sort of rationale. Marriage, he argues, is essentially more-than-rational, and cannot be justified in terms of finite reasons – 'every question as to its "why" is a misunderstanding which very easily lends itself to the ruminations of prosaic common sense' (EO 2, p. 62). He demolishes what he regards as the three most serious of the purported 'reasons' for marriage: that one marries because marriage is a school for character; that one marries in order to have children; that one marries in order to acquire a home; and he mentions, in passing, several less worthy reasons for marriage which are none the less to be encountered in modern society – 'for the sake of money, or from Jealousy, or for the sake of one's "prospects" . . .' (EO 2, p. 88).

On what, then, is marriage actually based? The Assessor puts it most succinctly in an essay on marriage which is included in *Stages on Life's Way*. Here – like the Romantics – he assigns to man and woman the respective polarities of spirit, sense, etc., but, he goes on to argue, these two halves are not sufficient of themselves to make a whole or to achieve a perfect union of souls. A third factor is needed, and this third factor he finds in resolution or choice, an act of will based on and guided by religious presuppositions. 'Resolution is a religious life-view constructed on ethical presuppositions, which equally smooths love's path and secures it against every outward and inward danger' (SLW, p. 162). Yet it would be a mistake to think of William's concept of resolution solely in terms of individual will-power: it is not a reiteration of Fichte's conception of the self-creating will, but depends on a fundamental openness to God. Resolution is, in Kierkegaard's vocabulary, a theological term. Marriage cannot be truly based on any 'finite why' but only on the resolution which is rooted in a faithful response to religious revelation. Resolution is the only language in which God and human beings can speak to each other.

There is an analogy between Kierkegaard's discussion of marriage and his treatment of politics, for here too we can discern the outlines of a characteristically Lutheran theological approach. Here marriage is seen as an ordinance of creation, 'instituted of God' but not of itself expressing the ideal of Christian perfection. Such ordinances, in the words of Emil Brunner, 'do not belong to the realm of redemption, the Church, but belong to the realm of divine preservation, in which all natural impulses and reason are constituent factors'.[2] In the same way that the strong arm of the state serves to restrain the worst excesses of sinfulness in the larger social order, so marriage serves, in the words of the Book of Common Prayer, as 'a remedy against sin' for those who 'have not the gift of continency'. From this perspective, marriage is not seen primarily as serving purely human ends, but can only be understood within the Christian framework of creation, fall and redemption. Once this framework has been abandoned marriage loses its essential authority and is reduced to being a kind of 'front' for the satisfaction of the purely egotistical desires of fallen man. The Romantic view of love, Kierkegaard believes, has committed just this error: it sees marriage solely from the standpoint of human self-fulfilment. But, says Kierkegaard, this is a deception, for it really means that marriage is based on selfishness. There is thus a yawning gulf between the Romantic 'ideal' of marriage based purely on love and the reality of the married state. In the light of this the Romantic mythology of love itself becomes a main cause of the disappointment and frustration which modern marriages so frequently experience.

> Generally it can be assumed that every married man is secretly mortified because he feels that he has been made a fool of when all this ravishing talk from the courting days, all this about Julie being the paragon of loveliness and beauty, and getting to possess her is the highest bliss turns out to be – a false alarm. This is the first knock the husband gets, but this in itself is not insignificant, because it is hard for a man to admit that he has been fooled, that both he and Julie must have been crazy. The next undermining is that the husband and Julie (who has incidentally had the same experience on her side) agree to keep a stiff upper lip and to hide things from others; they agree to tell the lie that marriage is the true happiness and that they especially are happy. (JP 4998)

'Julie', as Kierkegaard observes, is as much a victim of the deception of
the Romantic idealization of love as her husband – perhaps even more
so:

> If the girl is called Juliana, then her life runs like this: 'previously
> Empress in love's far-fetched hyperbole and titular Queen of all
> foolish exaggerations [she is] now Madame Petersen on the corner of
> Bath Street'. As a child a girl is less honoured than a boy. When she
> is a little older one doesn't rightly know what to do with her; finally
> comes that decisive period which makes of her a ruler. Adoringly,
> man approaches her as wooer ... He kneels, he adores, he speaks of
> his beloved in the most fantastic categories, and then he quickly
> forgets the kneeling position (and he knew very well while he was
> kneeling that it was a fantasy). If I were a woman I would rather be
> sold by my father to the highest bidder, for at least there is some
> meaning in a business deal. (SLW, pp. 57–8)

The modern age of reflection not only destroys the primitive capacity
for personal resolution in the sense described above, but it also vitiates
the sheer passion of genuine erotic love – 'Not even the immediacy of
love is in the present age as carefree as the lilies of the field or in the
lover's eyes more glorious than Solomon in all his glory' (TA, p. 75).
'Love', says Kierkegaard, 'like all passion, has become dialectical for
the present generation' (SLW, p. 407) – in other words, it is no longer
based solely upon the violence of immediate passion, but upon reflection, consideration, technique. Ritualized coquetry has replaced the
honest expression of real ardour, so much so that 'One cannot grasp
such an immediate passion, and even a grocer's boy would be able to
tell Romeo and Juliet amazing truths' (SLW, p. 407).

The damage which the reflective character of the modern age does to
the whole area of personal relationships is, in Kierkegaard's eyes,
nowhere more apparent than in the changing self-evaluation of
woman. Along with the Romantics he sees womanhood as essentially
embodying the values of immediacy: feeling, passion, emotion, etc., and
she thus comes to represent the hidden, nurturing, sustaining dimension
of life. She is that which roots man to the earth. The ontological
distinction between male and female roles is clearly expressed (on
Kierkegaard's behalf) by the Assessor William:

> Woman clarifies finitude, man chases after the infinite ... woman
> bears children with pain, but man conceives ideas with pain ...

because woman thus clarifies finitude she is therefore man's deepest
life, but a life which should be hidden and concealed as the life of a
root always is. (EO 2, p. 311)

For the Assessor, woman's long, voluptuous hair is a vivid symbol of
her profound earthliness and of how she binds man to the earth (EO 2,
pp. 312–13). Less poetically, Kierkegaard says bluntly that woman's
true vocation in life is 'homeliness', i.e. to provide a background for the
social transcendence of the male.

> There is an adjective which describes woman's essential character-
> istic ... This characteristic is: homeliness, woman's character, just as
> it is man's character to be a character ... Take a simple, plain
> woman – if it can truly be said of her that she is homely: all honour
> to her; I bow as low before her as before a Queen! And, on the other
> side, if the Queen does not have homeliness, then she is only a
> mediocre madam. (FSE/JY, p. 49)

Homeliness expresses itself above all in the capacity for silence, a
silence which functions as a creative counter-force to the busyness and
noisiness of man's tasks in work and in society.

In the modern age, however, woman is no longer content to be
defined in these terms, but seeks to mould her own life in what had been
traditionally regarded as the masculine categories of reflection. This
development seemed, to Kierkegaard, to be pregnant with disaster for
humanity, since it removed the last 'natural' bulwark against the
spreading quicksands of nihilism. He is very much with the Assessor
when he explodes: 'I hate all the disgusting talk about women's
emancipation. God forbid that it ever happens!' (EO 2, p. 311).

> For these days a girl learns so much at the Institute, French and
> German and Drawing; and at home she certainly learns many useful
> things. The question is whether these days she learns that which is
> most important of all: silence. I do not know ... Remember the
> apostle's word about beholding oneself in the mirror of the Word.
> For a woman who looks in the mirror a lot becomes vain and vainly
> talkative! Ah, and a woman who looks at her image in the mirror of
> the age becomes raucously noisy! (FSE/JY, p. 50)

Kierkegaard's concern that women are in the process of losing their
traditional qualities of 'homeliness' and 'silence' and being dragged into

the noisome vortex of modernity needs to be related to the overall structure of his critique of the present age and of its propensity to envy and idle chatter. It is not just a matter of keeping women in their place, but of securing an alternative reservoir of values to sustain humanity in the face of the nihilistic levelling tendencies of modern times. None the less it is clear that throughout his authorship he regarded women's emancipation as a particularly odious manifestation of the modern spirit.

Kierkegaard's very first published work had, in fact, been a short (and rather silly) satire on the emancipation of women, and he returned to the theme at various points in his work. There are many indications of his views both in *Either-Or* and in *Stages on Life's Way* (which includes a rather nasty but brilliant denunciation of the modern cult of fashion). At one time he planned a highly critical review of the novel *Clara Raphael*, regarded by many as one of the first examples of feminist literature in Scandinavia (JP 6709), and he firmly declined an invitation to meet Frederika Bremer, a leading Swedish feminist. It is, indeed, hard to imagine what they might have had to say to each other. In Kierkegaard's eyes the women's movement was a paradigm of the levelling spirit of envy and comparison, which could only serve to underline the fact that the private sphere of personal relationships was no longer capable of providing a real resource for the nurture and life of the spirit in the modern age. Without the organic complementarity of man and woman, received and accepted as a divine ordinance, love would degenerate from the status of a religious duty to the (romantically falsified) brutality of animal instinct and the selfish exploitation, the one of the other. So even here, in this most personal area of human experience, the age of reflection cripples and obscures the human capacity for truth and meaning.

It is curious that in the light of the sometimes extraordinarily misogynistic tone of Kierkegaard's writings about women, that many women commentators find a positive aspect to his discussion. Birgit Bertung has, for example, interpreted his written view of women in the light of the principle of indirect communication. As she sees the situation, Kierkegaard is saying to women, 'Look at what you have allowed society to make of you: wake up, and seize the spiritual identity that is your proper goal.'[3] Leading feminist theologians such as Dorothee Sölle have also acknowledged the positive impact on them of Kierkegaard's thought.[4]

The Church

Having dismissed the claims of politics and private life to provide 'answers' to the crisis of post-Enlightenment humanity, Kierkegaard would, if he were any ordinary apologist, proceed to bring forward religion as the sole authentic response to this otherwise unresolvable situation. Now there is indeed a sense in which it can be said that this is just what he does. However, the 'religion' which Kierkegaard has to offer is a very different matter from what customarily passes under that name. In his view, the sociological organization of the Church can no longer be regarded as capable of either containing or expressing the faith which saves. No more than any political organization can the Church claim to possess the 'fixed point' which would bring a halt to the vortex of nihilism, since the Church itself has been utterly permeated by the worldly, bourgeois, reflective spirit of the age.

We can find passages from just about the whole of Kierkegaard's authorship which would illustrate his understanding of the way the Church allowed itself to be manipulated by secularism, but his polemic against the Church was most forcibly expressed in a series of articles and pamphlets published in the last year of his life. Kierkegaard rarely expressed himself more clearly, with as few digressions and as few literary or logical red herrings, as in this last 'Attack upon "Christendom"'. He had, he said, in this whole business only one point to make, namely, that

> The Christianity of the New Testament just doesn't exist. There is nothing here to reform; all that matters is to shine a light on a 'Christian' criminal act which has been carried out over centuries by millions of more or less guilty people, an act by which they have cunningly sought, little by little, to trick God away from Christendom, and got Christianity to be quite the opposite of what it is in the New Testament. (KAUC, pp. 32–3)

He also pointed out with singular clarity the practical implications which resulted from the exposure of this 'criminal act'.

> Whoever you are, whatever the rest of your life may be, my friend, – by ceasing to take part in public worship (if, that is, you do take part in it) as it now is (i.e., claiming to be the Christianity of the New Testament) then you have permanently got one thing less to be guilty of, one very big thing: you do not take part in making a fool of God

by calling something New Testament Christianity which is not New Testament Christianity. (KAUC, p. 59)

He took his own advice and ceased attending public worship, and when asked on his deathbed if he wished to receive communion replied that he would only do so if it could be administered by a lay person (the method of paying the clergy being one of the chief themes of his attack) – which was not, of course, permitted. At the same time it has to be emphasized that he constantly reaffirmed his faith in God throughout the attack and during his final illness.

The occasion of this whole outburst was the death of J. P. Mynster, the Primate of the Danish Lutheran Church. Kierkegaard had known Mynster since his childhood, indeed the Bishop had been his father's priest and had prepared the young Kierkegaard for confirmation. Mynster had exercised a considerable spiritual authority in Danish church life for many years, and he was a deeply venerated man. His sermons reveal a strong, humane faith, influenced by the pietism of the eighteenth century, expressed in a clear but dignified style. Mynster was, in short, as much the incarnation of established religion – at its best – as a man could be. Even in the attack Kierkegaard acknowledged Mynster's greatness when he wrote of him that 'he bore a whole generation' (KAUC, p. 9). At the same time, however, he could write in a letter to Mynster's son: 'From the first time I spoke with him I told him privately and in as solemn terms as possible how much I disagreed with him' (LD, p. 417).

What moved him to make these private accusations public was a memorial sermon preached by H. L. Martensen, a churchman who had already incurred Kierkegaard's wrath on account of his Hegelian tendencies and who was now the leading candidate among Mynster's possible successors. In this sermon Martensen referred to the late bishop as a 'witness to the truth', an expression possibly coined by Kierkegaard, but which, in any case, had considerable significance for him and a very precise meaning. Kierkegaard meant by 'witness to the truth' one whose witness was like that of the martyrs of the early Church, that is, a witness in blood. Here is a part of one of his more vivid descriptions of such a witness:

A witness to the truth, that is, a man whose life from first to last is unacquainted with everything that is called enjoyment ... but on the contrary from first to last initiated into everything that is called suffering ... A witness to the truth, that is a man who witnesses to the truth in poverty, in poverty, lowliness and abasement, therefore misunderstood, hated, despised, therefore mocked, scorned and treated contemptuously – he was so poor that perhaps he did not always have his daily bread, but every day he richly received the daily bread of persecution ... A witness to the truth ... that is a man who is flogged, mistreated, dragged from one prison to another, and lastly ... crucified, or beheaded or burned or roasted on a gridiron, his lifeless body cast out by the executioner in a lonely place without burial ... or burnt to ashes and scattered to the winds so that every trace of this 'offscouring' (as the apostle called himself) might be eradicated. (KAUC, p. 7)

There is arguably a morbid element in this concept of the witness to the truth, an element which can be associated with Kierkegaard's negative attitude towards physicality in general, but at the same time the idea of testifying to Christ by poverty, suffering, etc., is a genuine part of the Christian tradition. It is amply evidenced in the New Testament itself, in the sub-apostolic literature and in many reform movements down the ages. It is an idea which has also regained something of its prominence in the storms of our own century, when Christianity has found itself in conflict with various forms of totalitarian repression. It was under such a regime that Dietrich Bonhoeffer wrote, 'When Christians are exposed to public insult, when they suffer and die for his sake, Christ takes on visible form in his Church.'[5] The extremity of Kierkegaard's way of expressing this idea of the blood-witness should not blind us to the truth that it is firmly rooted in a major strand of traditional Christian spirituality. What particularly incensed him was that this idea should be applied to a man like Mynster who 'was highly worldly-wise, but weak, self-indulgent, and only great as an orator ...' (KAUC, p. 9) and whose preaching 'soft-pedals, veils, is silent about and omits something most decisively Christian ...' (KAUC, p. 5).

Up until now we have seen Kierkegaard largely in the role of self-appointed defender of the established order against intellectual and political radicalism. Now, however, he seems to want to forge an alliance of convenience with the liberals and secularizers in their attack on the church establishment. The reason for this change of tack is not to be found in a late espousal of liberal principles, but, as has already been indicated, by the rigorous application of a concept which was provided by the Christian tradition itself. Indeed, he argued, it is a pattern we find in the life of Christ himself. Quite apart from his claim to be the 'God-man' (a claim Kierkegaard does not subject to historical scrutiny), his claim purely as an individual to qualify or to put aside the traditional commandments of the law created a collision between himself and the established order, a collision which Kierkegaard defines as the perennial 'collision between pietism and the established order' (PC, p. 86). 'Every time a witness to the truth makes truth into inwardness (and this is the essential business of a witness to the truth) ... then the established order will also be offended by him' (PC, p. 87). The reason for this offence is that the established order has an innate tendency to self-deification, a tendency Kierkegaard notes in the philosophy of Hegel and which he defines as

> ... the perpetual uprising, the constant rebellion against God. God wants ... to have a little bit of a hand in directing the development of the world, or maintaining the development of the race. But this is opposed by the deification of the establishment as the self-serving invention of the torpid worldly mind, which wants to lie down and rest and imagines that now we have perfect peace and security, now we have reached the highest point of development. (PC, p. 88)

The 'established order' which Kierkegaard attacks is therefore not at all to be identified with that primitive dimension of givenness which lies at the heart of faith and which is beyond criticism. It is far from being the divinely ordained power which it imagines itself to be: it is, Kierkegaard pointedly says, more like an ennobled bourgeois who seeks to erase the memory of his real origins. The ultimate repository of religious givenness is not to be found in the sociologically defined establishment but in the primitiveness of the individual religious personality.

Kierkegaard spelled out his own relation to Mynster (and through him to the establishment in general) in the following parable. Imagine, he wrote, a luxury liner out at sea. In the lounge the festivities are in full swing. Meanwhile, on the horizon is a white speck which indicates the advent of a terrible storm. The captain, however, instead of taking his place on the bridge, mingles jovially with the passengers and

> ... no one sees the white speck or suspects what it means. But no ... there is one person who sees it and knows what it means – but he is a passenger. He has, after all, no command on the ship; he cannot do anything. But in order to do the one single thing he can do, he asks the captain to come up on deck, only for a moment. It takes a while, but finally he comes – but does not wish to hear anything and, passing it off as a joke, hurries down to the noisy, hilarious company

in the lounge, where the toasts are being drunk to the captain with the usual enthusiasm, for which he thanks affably. In his anxiety the poor passenger decides to dare once again to inconvenience the captain, but this time he is even impolite to him. But the white speck is still there on the horizon: 'It will be a frightful night.' (JP 3069)

Kierkegaard, then, sees Mynster as being criminally blind to the devastating consequences for religion of the gathering storm of modern nihilism. And this parable also indicates another aspect of the 'witness to the truth'. The witness does not simply suffer (we all do that in any case, Kierkegaard believes) – he acts, as the captain in the story fails to act. Christianity is not a matter of giving intellectual assent to verbal propositions but is a challenge to live a special kind of life. It is a matter of life-view, not world-view. As such it is real only when it is lived. Part of the numbness of the established Church in the face of modernity is that it has allowed the fundamental ethical quality of faith to be dissolved into theory, and has accommodated Christianity to both philosophy and poetry, turning the question as to the truth of existential witness into a debate about opinions.

In this connection we are led to see another aspect of Kierkegaard's attack on Hegelianism. For the assimilation of Hegelianism by theologians was a clear sign to Kierkegaard that Christianity had misconstrued the relationship between theory and practice that was fundamental to its own truth. It is in the light of this that we must read the motto to *Philosophical Fragments*, in which Kierkegaard makes clear his view that there can be no common ground between Christianity and philosophical idealism. It reads simply: 'Better well hung than ill wed.' The marriage of Christianity with modern thought is, in this sense, a bad marriage.

The practical spirit of Christianity is not merely vitiated by this association with philosophy, it is also, in modern church life, transmuted into a kind of poetry. In his major self-assessment *The Point of View* Kierkegaard justifies his procedure of starting his authorship with largely 'aesthetic' works such as *Either-Or* by arguing that the good educator always starts where people actually are, and where the Christendom of the present age actually is is closer to the theatre than the confessional. Christianity has, under the aegis of the present establishment, become, in effect, theatre itself – with the difference 'that the theatre honestly and reasonably admits that it is what it is; the Church on the contrary is a theatre which in every way tries dishonestly to hide what it is' (KAUC, p. 197). The priest is no longer heard preaching with apostolic authority – for he has degenerated into a poet who, far from provoking an awareness of the seriousness of the human predicament, spreads a mild, soothing light across the scarred landscape of the man-made wilderness of the modern world.

> ... for it is surely a sign of sickness that the sick person desires most forcefully and loves most of all precisely that which is most harmful to him. But, in a spiritual sense, humanity in its natural state is sick, has gone astray, is self-deceived, and therefore desires most of all to be deceived, so as to get permission not only to continue straying, but also to really make itself at home in its self-deceit. And a deceiver suitable for this task is precisely – the poet. Therefore the human race loves him above all others. (KAUC, p. 201)

The priest of the modern state church is just such a poet. He is the spiritual child of the prophets who proclaimed peace when there was no peace, or who exhorted the Judaeans to rely on the holiness of the Temple rather than on obedience to the law.

The non-prophetic, non-apostolic, non-authoritative Church run by such 'poetic' priests is reduced to being an ideological instrument for the self-justification of the bourgeoisie. The real God of this Church is the common round of ordinary civic life in all its pettiness and banality. Like his clientèle, the priest puts seeking a living (a house, an income, etc.) before seeking the kingdom of God. He allows his course in life to be directed by his family and personal attachments rather than by conscience, and in his ministry he implicitly encourages the belief that simply by virtue of taking part in ordinary family life, men and women are fulfilling the requirements of the Christian life.

> The aim of 'priestly' Christianity is to use religion (which unfortunately is really for producing the opposite effect) to cement families more and more egotistically together, and to arrange family festivals, beautiful, glorious family festivals such as infant baptism and confirmation, which festivals, compared with outings to the Deer Park and other family amusements, have their own special magic in that they are 'also' religious. (KAUC, p. 222)

In short, he concludes, the priests serve much the same function in society as Carstensen, the manager of Copenhagen's Tivoli amusement park: perhaps, he muses, Carstensen too might be ordained ...

This whole *mésalliance* between Christianity and the family is seen by Kierkegaard as culminating in the mystification surrounding sexuality and procreation.

> Men seem to have a good many and very different preoccupations. But if one were to be named that could be called the one and only thing which preoccupies men, it would have to be: sex, sexual desire, propagation and the like: for, after all, men are primarily animal ... (JP 3966) ... In the sexual relation man is not on a level lower than the animal, but *au niveau*; and there is nothing further to be said on that, we are indeed animal creations. But what frequently makes man sink lower than the animal on this point is the nauseatingly hypocritical solemnity with which he refines this relation. (JP 3967)

In modern society it has become precisely the best-known function of the Church to provide this 'nauseatingly hypocritical solemnity' by means of baptism, confirmation and marriage services, which lull people into assuming that merely by indulging their animal instinct for self-propagation they are fulfilling the good and perfect will of God.

But what is the scope of this invective against the establishment? It began with an attack on a single expression in a single sermon, but soon widened into an attack on the whole of the Danish national church, beyond which Kierkegaard saw Protestantism in general. He seemed, however, to draw a distinction of principle between Protestantism and Catholicism in this respect. He regards Catholicism as being just as liable to degenerate into 'surface sanctity' as Protestantism is to fall into 'spiritless secularism', but, he says, look at the difference in this way:

> Imagine a completely secularized Catholic prelate [whose] whole life is all possible enjoyment beyond that of the most secularized worldly-shrewd Epicurean. Now, how will a Catholic judge him? ... the Catholic will easily see that this is worldliness. And why will he easily see this? Because Catholicism simultaneously expresses an entirely different aspect of Christianity in whose cause the high prelate must also acquiesce; side by side with him walks one who lives in poverty, and the Catholic has a pathos-filled conception of this which is sounder than the prelate's which, alas, is only worldliness. Now, on the other hand, imagine a Protestant country where there is no thought of Catholicism ... now imagine in this Protestant country there lived a high Protestant cleric, an exact counterpart of the Catholic prelate: what then? Well, the Protestant cleric has a refinement – ah, a refinement the Catholic prelate hankers after in

vain ... the refinement that his contemporaries understand his secular mentality and worldly enjoyment of life as – religiousness! (JP 3617)

Although this hardly amounts to an apology for Catholicism, it suggests that Catholicism, however corrupt, still maintains an authentically religious ideal – Protestantism, however, has made secularism itself a religion. Above all, Protestantism has abandoned the heart of real Christian piety – the call to imitate Christ. For Kierkegaard, Christ is not only to be construed as Saviour but also as the Pattern by which we are to live. It is not by external conformity to the 'rites and ceremonies' of established religion but by inward wrestling with the requirement of imitation – Follow me! – that we attain to the primitiveness in which we encounter the 'givens' that alone withstand the all-consuming forward march of nihilism. Radical discipleship is our last refuge. Paradoxically it is this very option which modern, secularized religion completely obscures. It is man's most invidious form of self-deception. The critique of religion both crowns and incorporates the other aspects of Kierkegaard's attack on the present age, for here the spirit of the age is fully operative and makes its most dangerous claim of all – not merely to be accepted as fate but to be honoured as God.

FOUR

CRITIQUE OF PHILOSOPHY
AND SCIENCE

———

The Scope of Kierkegaard's Critique
of Hegel

KIERKEGAARD'S ASSAULT ON the modern world embraced not only
the general character or 'spirit' of the age but also took in the major
social forms which he saw as serving the cause of nihilistic levelling. In
addition to this he also laid siege to the theoretical self-understanding
of the modern age and its cultural self-expression: in other words, in
relation to its philosophy and its art. In turning to examine his critique
of philosophy it is important to keep hold of the connection between
this and the overall thrust of his *Zeitkritik*. When Kierkegaard takes
issue with Hegelian philosophy it is not just because he has found one
or two inconsistencies in Hegel's philosophical arguments (although he
does not hesitate to enter into such details, as we shall see) but because
he finds that that philosophy taken as a whole embodies and articulates
the fundamental presuppositions of modern nihilism. Like so many
Marxist critics of Hegelianism (from whom he would of course differ
on almost every other point) Kierkegaard sees in Hegelianism the
supreme self-expression of the bourgeois world-order. But there is
more. For his analysis of the specific failings of Hegelian idealism leads
him to identify a faultline running through the whole tradition of
philosophizing in the West since the Greeks – and not just in
philosophy in the narrow sense but in the whole way in which we
relate to and construe reality. The critique of Hegelianism in Kierkegaard's writings is therefore more than just another argument among
philosophers: it raises fundamental questions as to the present and
future shape of human thinking. When the philosopher Martin Heidegger was asked for a contribution to the 1963 UNESCO symposium
on Kierkegaard's thought, he entitled his paper 'The End of Philosophy
and the Task of Thinking'. Although Heidegger made it clear on a
number of occasions that he did not regard Kierkegaard as a major
metaphysical thinker, he did see in his work an epochal symptom that

marked the beginning of the end of a tradition of thinking that ran all the way back to Plato. What might it mean to see Kierkegaard's critique of Hegel as part of such a grand strategy?

Hegel shared with his philosophical contemporaries of the early nineteenth century an acute awareness of the predicament of the 'divided self' of the modern world, and their various philosophies were, in their different ways, attempts to bring about a new sense of unity and cohesion. For the Hegelians it was the process of philosophy itself which provided the principal means of curing the sickness of the age. One of Hegel's Danish admirers, the playwright and critic J. L. Heiberg (ridiculed by Kierkegaard in the anecdote in the *Concluding Unscientific Postscript* about the miraculous conversion to Hegelianism of Dr Hjortespring), offered an effective popularization of this view in a pamphlet aptly titled *On the Meaning of Philosophy for the Present Age*. Heiberg suggested that the present age was one of continual crisis in which not only religion, but also poetry and art had lost their former power to convey 'immediate certainty concerning the divine and eternal' and that it was consequently left to philosophy to heal the self-inflicted wounds of the Enlightenment. But what did the Hegelians mean by philosophy?

In the programmatic preface to his *The Phenomenology of Spirit*, Hegel had distanced himself from the position taken by his former friend and colleague, the Romantic philosopher F. J. W. Schelling. Schelling's view was that man's apprehension of the Absolute occurs principally in a kind of 'aesthetic intuition' and that therefore poetry and art are the most appropriate forms in which to express this apprehension. Not so, protested Hegel, for truth cannot be based on a mere intuition since it both depends on and demands the systematic, scientific and conceptually precise investigation of the total process (natural, psychological and historical) by which consciousness has arrived at its present state. 'The true is the whole', he wrote.[1] Moreover, 'the true shape in which truth exists can only be the scientific system of such truth'.[2] Philosophy, then, is ultimately the exposition of the ways in which the world comes to be what it is and of the ways by which we come to know it to be so. Rationality and reality coincide so that scientific philosophy is simply the expression of the rationale of the real. Science, here, it should be noted, means something much wider than 'science' in English usage. The German word *Wissenschaft* does not just relate to the natural sciences but applies to any subject which is approached in an organized, deliberate and rational way, so that it is as normal to speak of the 'human sciences' (*Geisteswissenschaften*) as of the natural sciences (*Naturwissenschaften*). Science in this sense is – or should be – the basic form of all work carried out in universities and in higher education generally.

Ironically enough, Hegel's own method, which attempted to trace the development of both reality and of human thought about reality by means of an a priori pattern of logical relationships, fares very poorly in the light of more recent concepts of scientific thinking. The empiricist tradition, for example, tends to see Hegel as an outstanding example of the arrogant pseudo-scientific spirit which tries to make facts fit theories rather than submit to the patient discipline of controlled observation. Kierkegaard's own critique of Hegel contains similar elements, as we shall see. But perhaps even Hegel's empiricist critics would accept his intention of presenting the findings of knowledge in a coherent, consistent and systematic way, even if their idea of systematic thought is more open-ended than his. What Hegel was striving for was to give knowledge an objective form, to let its rationality be seen, to expose it to argument and refutation rather than to take refuge in the beautiful but vacuous assertions of the Romantics.

How different is this aim from that enshrined in the organization of any typical modern research project? Heidegger's account of contemporary research is highly illuminating in this respect for he argues that modern science, although it does not regard itself as idealist, is in fact, only prepared to allow any event or phenomenon to count as 'real' when the parameters of its reality have been established by a programme of rigorously executed research. The only truth worth considering is the truth which can be established and presented scientifically and systematically, without coming into contradiction with either itself or with other data of knowledge that have already been independently 'proven'. Heidegger suggests that such modern research is the culmination of a very long-term historical process originating in humanity's stepping back from the totality of the world in such a way as to 'picture' the world over against it and simultaneously experiencing itself as a spectating subject. This, he argues, is something typically 'modern'. Neither the Greeks nor the Middle Ages had a world-picture in this sense, and its emergence indicates the subjection of the realm of nature, of whatever is simply 'given', to man-made ends and purposes. Science and knowledge thus inevitably spill over into technology, or, rather, they are themselves aspects of what is fundamentally a technocratic approach to reality. The very structure of science – as it has been practised in the West – is, according to Heidegger, shaped by the purpose of gaining mastery over that which is.[3]

This suggests something of the scope of Kierkegaard's critique of Hegel. For what is at stake in that critique is much more than the truth or falsity of a set of arguments entertained by a certain number of professional philosophers in the privacy of their studies: what is at stake is the very conception of thinking and of rationality which underpins the relationship of humanity to its environment and its history. None the less, the sphere of philosophy in the narrow sense provided Kierkegaard with an excellent focus by which to see what was going on in this wider field, and it is to his narrowly philosophical objections to 'the system' that we now turn.

The Question of Doubt

In his epochal *Discourse on Method*, René Descartes described how he resolved to seek an unshakeable ground for truth by regarding as 'absolutely false everything in which I could suppose the slightest reason for doubt, in order to see if there did not remain after that anything in my belief which was entirely indubitable'.[4] In this respect Hegel saw himself as the inheritor of Descartes, only, he believed, he took this principle of methodical doubt considerably further than Descartes had done. Playing on the etymological link between doubt (Ger. = *Zweifel*) and despair (Ger. = *Verzweiflung*) Hegel calls his own procedure a 'way of despair',[5] that is, a further intensification of doubt. Contrasting with his own brand of radical scepticism the Enlightenment principle 'not to give oneself over to the thoughts of others, upon mere authority but to examine everything for oneself and follow only one's own conviction', Hegel propounded a critical approach which would be directed against 'the whole range of phenomenal consciousness'.[6]

Thus whereas Descartes was able, to his own satisfaction at least, to establish the principle of *cogito ergo sum* ('I think, therefore I am') as an absolutely unquestionable basis for knowledge, Hegel went on to doubt the forms of the thinking consciousness itself, and to dissolve all mental phenomena (including such axiomatic 'truths' as Descartes' 'Cogito') into a process of becoming, an all-embracing relativity. Consciousness, he asserts, cannot be 'proved' to be valid by means of such an abstract principle, but has to be explained in the light of the total historical process by which it has reached its present condition. By analysing this history we discover the basic dialectical laws which govern the movement of the whole. In fact, for Hegel, this dialectical structure involves a continually repeated act of negation, such that each new stage of consciousness emerges only as the specific negation of the preceding stage. For example, the Christian faith in the incarnation of the Godhead in the physical body of an individual man can only be understood in relation to the foregoing pagan idea of the realm of the gods as existing outside or beyond the world of man. The Greek mythology, with its depiction of gods in human form, has, in its turn, to be understood as a negation of the Egyptian cultus of god in animal or mixed human-animal form, and this transition is concretely embodied in the story of Oedipus and the Sphinx.

In Hegel's view each stage or moment thus presents one aspect of the truth, which emerges in its fullness only when the modern scientific and historical consciousness grasps the whole series of stages in its totality. Thus the negative dialectic of consciousness leads to a positive vision of truth in the whole, which Hegel calls 'the negation of the negation'. In other words, if we press doubt far enough, we will win through to a positive view of truth. Cartesian doubt, the doubt of one-sided rationalism, is merely negative, destroying dogma and under-mining prevailing superstitions and prejudices of all kinds, whereas Hegel's doubt is presented as, in the last resort, self-negating, so that we end with a new positivity. This alone, and not any reversion to naive intuitionism, is the way to truth. What 'doubt' means in this context is essentially the same as 'reflection' (in Hegel's sense). Doubt/reflection is the tool by which philosophy breaks up the complacency of 'immediacy', the realm of whatever can be known by empirical observation, the 'real world' of unexamined common sense. The dialectic of consciousness can thus be seen as a journey from imme-diacy in this sense through reflection to a 'return' to immediacy, in which the world is once more seen in its real solidity yet is no longer merely 'seen' but understood.

Against Hegel, Kierkegaard argues that there is a fundamental discrepancy between the use of doubt as a method and the claim to have arrived at positive results. For Kierkegaard the 'negation of the negation' does not lead to a new positivity but leads us still further into the mire of negation. Once the primordial act of reflection has cut mind loose from its anchoring in immediate reality, there is no way by which mind itself can establish a 'new immediacy'. Once what Kierkegaard calls the 'self-reflective scepticism of thought' has been let loose it cannot, he believes, be brought to a halt except by a more than merely intellectual decision to acknowledge some transcendent fact or reality outside the critical consciousness itself. 'How can we bring this scepticism to a halt', he asks,

> which is based on thinking that selfishly wants to think about itself, instead of making itself serviceable by thinking some definite content? When a horse runs away and bolts ... someone might well say, 'Just let it run, it will soon get tired.' But that can't be said with regard to thought's reflection on itself, because that can go on as long as may be, and still keep running wild. (CUP I, p. 335)

Over against such scepticism Kierkegaard defends (or at least prefers) Schelling's claim that knowledge must ultimately be grounded on some kind of intuition in which the being of a reality other than mind itself is apprehended in a self-authenticating way. In, with, and under every act of consciousness we have an immediate intuition of the existence of the object towards which consciousness is directed. This assumption in favour of the being of the world is something we simply cannot get behind or beyond. Scepticism, however, brings this assumption into question and then, as in Descartes' formulation of the Cogito, tries to find a new ground for being on the basis of logic. For Hegel logic is thus not merely a way of thinking about things, but actually determines the way in which things are in themselves. But although Hegel dismisses Schelling's doctrine of the intellectual intuition, the 'method' with which he replaces it is, in the end, little more than conjuring with words. According to Hegel, Kierkegaard says,

> Self-reflection continues until it transcends itself, thought triumphally forces its way through and once more attains reality, the identity of thought and being is won in the realm of pure thought. But what does it mean to say that self-reflection continues until it transcends itself? It does not take long to discover the fraudulent element in self-reflection, but on the other hand, for however long it takes, one is caught up in the fraud. What does it mean to say 'until'? This is nothing but specious talk, which tries to corrupt the reader's imagination by means of sheer quantity, as if it made it easier to understand how self-reflection transcends itself, if we suppose it as happening over a long time. This quantitative approach is a counterpart to the infinitely small angles assumed by astronomers, which eventually become so small that we can call them parallel lines. The story about self-reflection continuing 'until, etc.', distracts attention from the dialectically main point: *how* is self-reflection transcended? (CUP I, pp. 335–6)

For Kierkegaard it is axiomatic that reflective thought and reality are qualitatively different in the sense that we cannot argue from one to the other, but can only relate them if we make an unprovable assumption in favour of their ultimate unity. Consciousness, he argues, does in fact continually make this assumption, and embraces the subject, the object and the relationship between them in a threefold unity. This can be exemplified, he suggests, in the very way we speak about consciousness, when we say, 'I (= subject) am conscious (= relationship) of that (= object)' (cf. PF/JC, p. 168). Thought and reality, subject and object do belong together in a relationship which is given and precedes all argument. Reflection, however, tries to abstract from this relationship and to determine the connection between subject and object from the perspective of subjective thought, a bias which is apparent in the very rationalism of Enlightenment thought. It is this unjustifiable bias he lays at the door of the Hegelians.

He does not, though, imagine that we can return to the naivety of the pre-critical outlook. What we have to do, he says, is to pursue doubt further, although not in the same way as Hegelianism does. What we need to see is that scepticism not only undermines our immediate confidence in the reality of the external world, but in the end leads to the dissolution of the very subject of consciousness. The outcome of a rigorously pursued programme of doubt is not the achievement of an objective system of knowledge but the absolute negativity in which all 'givenness' is cast aside. The real result of methodical doubt is thus not the system but the nihilism of the left-wing Hegelians such as Feuerbach and Strauss, and their systematic demolition of all preceding forms of thought and social order.

Kierkegaard's view of the scope of modern scepticism is illuminated by his Master's thesis *On the Concept of Irony*. This is largely a study of Socrates, in which Kierkegaard identifies irony as the fundamental characteristic both of Socrates' method and of his 'results'. Using this definition he draws a line between what properly belongs to Socrates in the Platonic dialogues and what Plato has added. Plato, he argues, pads out Socrates' ironic conclusions (or rather lack of conclusions) with his own (more or less poetical) positive teachings.

> Fantasy grows weary of the labour of dialectics and lays itself down to dream, and out of this proceeds the mythical ... the mythical is thus fantasy's enthusiasm placed in the service of speculation, and to a certain degree, what Hegel calls the pantheism of fantasy. (CI, p. 101)

Such fantasy presents a mythical view of the world of Ideas as a world somehow conceivable under the forms of time and space, whereas Socratic (and all other genuine) dialectics culminates in an altogether abstract or else a negative result. Dialectics is the pursuit of truth: mythology is the claim to possess it.

Kierkegaard goes on to identify a further stage in the development of philosophical mythology which occurs when it is perceived that the myth is not in itself sufficient to express the transcendent content of the Idea concealed within it. Myth is now understood as a mere picture or image of the Idea rather than as a complete embodiment of it. Myth is reduced to allegory. However, this process can operate in reverse. In a rationalistic age such as ours, reason may on occasion avail itself of mythological images or models by which to illustrate abstract, non-representational concepts. This use of images can, in certain thinkers, lead to a new mythologizing of consciousness, in which the pursuit of conceptual clarity is abandoned in favour of the poetic impact of the myth. Kierkegaard gives as an example of this the Romantic philosophy of Nature, in which the search for exact, verifiable knowledge of the world is given up to make room for a ravishingly beautiful but ultimately non-informative myth.

Socrates, for his part, kept himself poised at the apex of ironic consciousness without slipping into mythology. Standing between two different intellectual ages, he understood that the values and beliefs of the preceding age had lost their force while at the same time the forms which truth was to take in the coming age had not yet been revealed. Socrates therefore makes no claim to offer any positive teaching. His standpoint is one of 'infinite absolute negativity'. Such an ironic stance will be encountered wherever there is a major transition in human consciousness, and Kierkegaard gives various examples of such irony in the period of transition from the medieval to the renaissance world. What concerns him more directly, however, is the cult of irony in German Romanticism. What he objects to here is that instead of accepting a purely critical role this modern form of irony attempts to establish itself as a creative force and assumes what Kant would have called a constitutive role. The result of this error is either that irony loses itself in the creation of a new mythology (as in Romantic philosophy of Nature) or that it takes on a political form in the negative anti-establishment attitudes of the avant-garde.

Kierkegaard thus saw Romantic irony as the root of modern nihilism – a position his mentor Poul Martin Møller had already stated. Hegel tried to bring Romantic irony into line, but failed, in Kierkegaard's view, because he too made exactly the same presupposition in favour of scepticism. Any positive teaching which Hegel arrives at, supposedly on the basis of his negative dialectic, can therefore be nothing more than mythology – unless it is based on empirical observation surreptitiously slipped in to the system without being processed through the dialectical machinery of doubt. The supposed finality of the system is thus no more than an intellectual fantasy. 'In a speculative-fantastic sense and in an aesthetic-fantastic sense we have a positive conclusion in the system and in the fifth act of the drama, but such a conclusion only convinces fantastic beings' (CUP I, p. 121).

The philosophical question of the misrelation between methodical doubt and systematic results reflects Kierkegaard's view that bourgeois society, while claiming to be a society based on laws objectively grounded in the world order, is actually a society which rests on the negative consciousness of man in revolt. It is a world-historical attempt to found society on the arbitrary self-assertion of the collective human subject, to mould the world into humanity's image and likeness. Far from 'answering' the problem posed by this Promethean phenomenon, Hegel merely reflects it.

But, we might ask, does philosophy stand or fall with Hegel? Surely Hegel represents only one philosophical position among many – might there not be some other philosophy or world-view which could show us a better way? To answer these questions we have now to pursue Kierkegaard's critique of Hegel one stage further and see how the attack on Hegel's epistemology leads him to formulate a thorough-going distinction between theory and reality, a distinction which sets a limit to any philosophical attempt to determine man's place in the world.

Logic and Reality

In the *Concluding Unscientific Postscript*, the most referenced source for Kierkegaard's strictly 'philosophical' arguments and views, Kierkegaard refers to Lessing's dictum that if God were to hold all truth in his right hand and in his left the unending urge to seek truth, he (Lessing) would, without hesitation, choose the left, even if this entailed the necessity of occasionally falling into error. Commenting on this, Kierkegaard propounds two theses: firstly, that a logical system is possible; secondly, that an existential system is impossible. Existence, he asserts, can never be held by the all-too-narrow nets of logical categories. Logic can successfully establish a coherent system only by leaving out everything which belongs to existence. This is evident from the purely hypothetical character of logical relations.

In making this distinction between logic and reality Kierkegaard acknowledges his debt to the German Aristotle scholar, Adolf Trendelenburg. Trendelenburg went against the post-Kantian philosophical consensus in Germany by arguing that all knowledge must be rooted in sensory intuition. Thought may well be the mirror in which reality is reflected, he allows, but 'the law of reflection is not solely determined by the mirror'.[7] How, he asks, can judgements concerning the application of the modal categories of actuality, possibility and necessity be given by pure thought, as idealism claims? Logic can indeed form a self-contained system – but this system tells us nothing about the real world 'outside'.

Of fundamental importance to both Trendelenburg and Kierkegaard is the Hegelians' misuse of the concept of motion. Hegel argued that starting from purely logical definitions we are able to unravel a chain of necessary relationships by which the whole world of phenomenal being is supported and ordered. For instance, from the concept of Being we are led to postulate the counter-concept of Nothingness. From the interaction between these two concepts we are led to postulate the concept of motion. This basic pattern is the dialectical spur which sets the whole system in motion. But, objects Trendelenburg, 'pure Being is unmoved, nothingness ... is likewise unmoved. How then does a movement of Becoming come out of the unity of two unmoving representations?'[8]

Kierkegaard connects this discussion with Aristotle's concept of the transition from a state of possibility to a state of actuality which Aristotle calls kinesis. 'Hegel', he says, 'has never done justice to the category of transition. It would be significant to compare it with the Aristotelian teaching about kinesis' (JP 260). As Hegel sees it, the system moves uninterruptedly from its logical starting-point to its culmination in Absolute Science. The process of Being which the system is meant to reflect is a continuum, and it is in this sense that Kierkegaard refers to Hegel's philosophy as a philosophy of 'immanence'. There is no intrusion of any new quality, there is no transcendence; everything is qualitatively commensurable with everything else in the system and all change is thus purely quantitative. But, objects Kierkegaard, the transition from a hypothetical, logical formula to a real, existential state of affairs involves just such a qualitative change – the change from possibility to actuality. The fact that something actually is, actually comes into existence, cannot be explained logically.

The movement from logic to reality involves a leap. The system tries to mediate every concept, to confine reality within a logical continuum, but this, says Kierkegaard, is to fly in the face of facts. Existence is inescapably contingent. Reality can only be conceived as determinate, fixable, necessary, objectifiable when it is construed as something past, something over and done with. There may very well be a system of existence from the point of view of God, but not from the point of view of the human subject, who is utterly immersed in the stream of time, poised between past and future at every moment of his existence. What will occur cannot be deduced from the categories of thought alone. The basic dishonesty of Hegelianism is indicated by Trendelenburg again when he discusses Hegel's attempt to deduce the concept of Spirit from the concept of Nature, while at the same time claiming that Spirit, as essential freedom, is somehow 'higher' than Nature. According to Trendelenburg, this is in no way 'a step made by the self-moving dialectic but an imaginative leap effected by the hand of an audacious use of language'.[9]

It is at this point that we have to remind ourselves of Kierkegaard's basic ethical and religious concern in this argument. Although to a certain extent his discussion of logic and existence suggests that he would have subscribed to some kind of empiricism with regard to knowledge of the natural world, it is not with knowledge of this sort that he is primarily concerned. The real offence of the system is that, by leaving no room for transcendence, for qualitative change or for newness, it rules out the possibility of ethics, and thereby excludes the possibility of radical freedom. Freedom cannot be deduced from Nature or any other presupposed idea, but consists in a leap by virtue of which something new happens in the world. From the point of view of freedom even empirical or historical facts provide only 'raw material' out of which the free subject himself determines what is to count as meaningful in terms of his own life-view. Distinguishing between 'interested' and 'disinterested' knowledge, Kierkegaard argues that only ethical knowledge is truly 'interested', for only the ethical life-view is really concerned to bring about through action that which it postulates as its ideal. Facts culled from the realm of empirical or historical reality are, in this connection, as much the expression of a 'disinterested' attitude as the tautological truths of logic or mathematics. The scientist or the historian cannot affect the reality of the objects under investigation – but in a situation of ethical choice this is precisely what we have to do: to abstract an interpretation from the given reality of the situation and then to act on the basis of this interpretation. In terms of Kierkegaard's philosophical shorthand, the movement is one from Being (*Esse*) to possibility (*Posse*) and then back to Being.

This last movement, from possibility to actuality, is one aspect of what Kierkegaard calls 'repetition', a concept to which he devoted one of his most genial books. 'Repetition', he states, 'is freedom's task ... it signifies freedom itself, consciousness raised to its second potency ... the interest of metaphysics and furthermore the interest on which metaphysics is shipwrecked ...' (FT/R, p. 324). Metaphysics strives towards the idea of freedom, but is inadequate in its own terms (which are those of disinterested knowledge) to find an adequate expression for it. Repetition can only come about through the unfathomable activation of freedom itself in the existing subject.

With regard to the specific content of Christian freedom, Kierkegaard defines its object as the paradox. 'Philosophy's idea is mediation – Christianity's, the paradox' (JP 3072).

The Paradox

The concept of the paradox, like that of the leap of faith, is one of the key terms associated with the name 'Kierkegaard' in the history of ideas. Indeed it is the culmination of Kierkegaard's wrestling with the question of the relationship between logic and existence, possibility and actuality, and with the concepts of motion, of kinesis, and repetition in the light of a fundamental concern with the idea of human freedom, conceived in its full radicality and unpredictability. It is therefore worth giving some consideration to it – in particular to the question as to whether Kierkegaard's use of it requires us to discard all rational criteria in the realm of religious truth. However, in the present context of Kierkegaard's critique of philosophy it is important to note that only one aspect of the paradox comes into view. The full meaning of Kierkegaard's specific concept of paradox only emerges when we pay due attention to two further elements in it: firstly, the content given to faith by Christian doctrine and, secondly, the existential structure of human life. In other words, I am only concerned now with what might be called its formal aspect.

There is some evidence that Kierkegaard does not wish us to regard the paradox as necessarily opposed to reason. It is interesting to note that in one passage in his journals Kierkegaard connects his idea of the paradox to Leibniz's distinction between what is above and what is against reason. Leibniz's position, according to Kierkegaard, is that

Faith is above reason. By reason he understands, as he says in many places, a linking together of truths (*enchainement*), a conclusion from causes. Faith therefore cannot be proved, *demonstrated*, *comprehended*, for the link which makes a linking together possible is missing, and what else does this say than that it is a paradox. (JP 3073)

As that which is 'above' though not necessarily 'against' reason, the realm of the paradox is a sphere of existence which cannot be measured in terms of the systematic grid of calculable, mutually mediated concepts and arguments. Yet there is also a sense in which it can even be said to be not merely compatible with thought but its real fulfilment. 'This, then, is the highest paradox of thought: to want to discover something that cannot itself be thought. This passion of thought is basically present in all thought ...' (PF/JC, p. 37).

Why should this be so? One reason is that if thought is not directed to what transcends it, then we are back in the situation of Hegelian scepticism. When reason allows validity only to that which conforms to its own criteria, it is operating with an implied scepticism. To speak of what is given to reason as its 'raw material', or of what is beyond reason as the implied object of its ratiocinations as 'the paradox', is, then, to draw attention to the fact that reason is always already contextualized. There is no absolute presuppositionless beginning, for reason is a late arrival in the world of real actions and events.

Kierkegaard would therefore seem to be making a point akin to Paul Tillich's insistence that reason is ultimately 'ecstatic', always pointing beyond itself into the realm of being which is before and beyond thought.

For Kierkegaard, however, it is important to note that that to which thought points in pointing beyond itself is not 'being' in some metaphysical sense, but the actuality of a specific form of existence. The content of the paradox is necessarily factical, concrete, unique. This is indicated by a fundamental question running through both the *Philosophical Fragments* and the *Concluding Unscientific Postscript*: whether it is possible to have a historically specific point of departure for an eternal consciousness – or whether the hope of eternal blessedness can be based on historical knowledge? Kierkegaard takes this question from Lessing. Lessing himself denied the possibility of basing 'knowledge' of things eternal on the specific data of history, thereby attacking the position of those Protestant dogmatists who sought to tie knowledge of God and human salvation to the historically particular content of biblical revelation. Lessing sarcastically commented that such a possibility could only occur by means of a 'leap', a leap he confessed himself unable to make. Kierkegaard accepts Lessing's distinction between reason and revelation but interprets it in a quite opposite manner. Affirming that salvation does depend on the specifics of history he accepts the consequence that it can only be attained by virtue of a leap which goes beyond reason.

Kierkegaard is therefore at one with later existentialists such as Sartre for whom neither thought nor freedom can exist outside what Merleau-Ponty called the 'envelopment' or 'situation' of irreducible singularity. The human drive towards freedom and perspicuous self-knowledge is haunted and burdened by its unavoidable existential contingency and opacity.

'Hegelian necessity was not negated,' Sartre wrote of Kierkegaard,

> but it could not be embodied without becoming a singular and opaque contingency; in an individual the rationality of History is experienced irreducibly as madness, as an inner accident, expressive of random encounters. To our questioning, Kierkegaard replies by revealing another aspect of the paradox: there can be no historical absolute that is not rooted in chance; because of the necessity of anchorage, there can be no incarnation of the universal other than in the irreducible opacity of the singular.[10]

This contingency refers us simultaneously to the very particular circumstances of the subject's own life-story and also to that which he encounters in and through others as the forms by which to give value and a more-than-individual sense to his own individuality. Sartre the atheist thus curiously concedes a justifiable consistency to Kierkegaard in the latter's assertion that human freedom is not just rooted in the subjectivity of the individual as such, but springs from the relationship between the particular individual and the equally particular story enshrined in the Christian proclamation. The paradox, in short, has for its content not being-in-general, but the unique existence of Jesus Christ, a man utterly immersed in the normal accidents of historical life, and the relation of the equally particular believer who believes in him by making the leap of faith.

Although Kierkegaard would probably not have been averse to such a critique in its own terms, the doctrine of the paradox does not just serve to limit the false universality of idealism in the way that, for example, empirical science might. More important to Kierkegaard was the way in which idealism undermined the necessary conditions of ethical life and ethical self-understanding. The real thrust of his critique of the system is that it has no ethics and therefore no religion, since religion is permeated by the ethical concern for realizing the subject's capacity for freedom and responsibility. On this point Kierkegaard's critique would apply to other theoretical models of life in addition to idealism. For even if theory bases itself on observation rather than logic, as theory it is implicitly biased towards the superiority of knowledge over existence, a bias that is fatal to ethical life. Thus it has become commonplace to distinguish between the realm of scientifically established facts and the realm of moral decisions. Science, we are told, can only give us data – it cannot determine how we are to employ this data in the pursuit of our freely chosen tasks in life: the discoveries of science are neither good nor evil in themselves – everything depends on the use we make of them. But this, for Kierkegaard (and perhaps increasingly for contemporary humanity living in a situation where it is science itself that generates the most intractable ethical dilemmas), is precisely the issue. For it is in the ethical realm that it gets decided what meaning, what value, what purpose life is to have for us as personally existing human beings. It may well be that in the actual course of research science has to put such questions to one side, but if it then goes on, either practically or even in principle, to dismiss this ethical sphere as meaningless or secondary it becomes guilty of the same error with which Kierkegaard charges Hegel: it leaves out the one thing needful, repressing life for the sake of theory. But such theory can no longer pretend to be 'value-free'. It is rather itself a surreptitious mode of power, a way of exerting the dominion of knowledge and of rational control over the given reality which encompasses and permeates both the earth and humanity's own being. It actually itself proclaims a (concealed) ethical choice about what is to count as really human. Kierkegaard's critique of Hegel serves to prevent any premature resolution of this underlying question. Whereas the system comes to rest in an eternally reposeful state of self-contemplation, the ethical demand to embrace the paradox and to achieve repetition means that for the ethical individual life will always be a persistent striving, a process of becoming which has no end this side of eternity. An ethical choice is never a choice that has been made: it is always a choice waiting to be made. Neither philosophy nor science can make this choice for us.

What Kierkegaard is doing here, then, is not merely to distinguish the realm of human or moral science from the realm of natural science, nor to state a preference for one field of *Wissenschaft* over another, but to distinguish science as such, humanistic, social and natural, from the demands and exigencies of ethical life. When we move from science to life, we have to be prepared for a radical change of key and to call into question the presupposition 'that the meaning of human life must be conceivable within the meaning of the universe' (Schweitzer). If it is the case that previous views of ethics have been 'towed along' behind our world-views, the rise of science has made this procedure questionable. For, after Darwin, the universe can no longer be viewed in an optimistic-ethical way as providentially designed to facilitate the accomplishment of human purposes. It follows – *pace* the claims of biological ethics – that we have to abandon any attempt to deduce the values by which we live from a pre-existent world-view or general understanding of the way things are. 'This renunciation of world-view in the old sense, that is, of a unitary world-view which is complete in itself, means a painful experience for our thought,' wrote Albert Schweitzer over seventy years ago, '... but we must surrender to facts.'[11] It is a similar renunciation that Kierkegaard, writing eighty years before Schweitzer, asks us to make. Yet it is still by no means clear that this renunciation has been made or even that the issue has been resolutely faced. Even though the modern Western world eschews monistic philosophies in principle, in practice there are still a great many unitary world-pictures jostling for attention, a great many philosophical, religious, scientific and political hold-alls, claiming deliverance from the immense uncertainty that a truthful recognition of the power of nihilism brings with it. But, Kierkegaard tells us, it is precisely such unitary world-views that feed nihilism, since they sever the link with contingent reality that is the one real basis for all authentic moral and religious life.

Does Kierkegaard's concept of 'paradox' then come to this: a regulative concept, alerting us to the necessarily provisional nature of all theoretical considerations in the face of the urgency, the singularity and the situatedness of ethical decision-making, a warning that we must at all costs avoid smuggling 'world-view' into 'life-view' and giving our free, responsible decisions the authority of a presupposed agreement as to the nature of things?

To conclude thus might seem to weaken the sense of the paradox, and make it seem as if Kierkegaard were merely using extravagant language to remind us of what seem to be quite common and even quite vulgar beliefs about the relationship between theory and practice. Kierkegaard might not object too strongly to such a charge, but what he could very well say – quite forcibly – in reply, is that although lip-service is indeed frequently paid to the limitations of theory with regard to ethical practice, our practice still, generally, shows itself to be excessively theory-laden. Moreover, as well as casting a suspicious eye on all who claim to have put theory in its place, Kierkegaard does seem to be making a still stronger point: that the very specific nature of Christian ethical demands, demands defined by belief in the incarnate and crucified God as both ground of salvation and model for imitation, not only go beyond reason: they potentially overthrow all preconceptions as to the nature of the good life. The Christian paradox not only requires faith – it also risks offence. But to see how and why that should be so, we need to see the place of the paradox in the context of the development of the individual's ethical and religious life, a task to which we shall return in a later chapter.

FIVE

CRITIQUE OF ART

AS AN ALTERNATIVE to the worlds of philosophy and science, Western culture has long looked to that dimension of life and experience which we call art, and it might seem natural that in the light of his critique of philosophy and science Kierkegaard should turn to art, to aesthetic experience in the widest sense, to provide the sense of meaning and vitality which is lost in the objectifying rigours of science. Indeed, in the last two centuries there have been many who have explicitly claimed for aesthetic experience the task of defending man's primitivity in the face of the encroachments of rationalism. Arturo Fallico, an existentialist philosopher of art, expressed a widely felt attitude when he wrote that it is only in art that we are able to find the 'will to resist the nihilism which stealthily destroys the very soul of modern man ... the aesthetic attitude is the archenemy of the impersonal, the levelling, the non-purposive'.[1] In a similar vein Nietzsche argued that while science compels us to adopt a vision of reality which is fundamentally nihilistic, 'truth does not count as the supreme value, even less as the supreme power. The will to illusion, to deception, to becoming and change ... here counts as more profound, primeval ...'[2] This 'will' is what is revealed in the artist. Art is illusory – but it is an illusion which enhances and affirms our sense of meaning and value. 'Art and nothing but art! It is the great means of making life possible, the great seduction to life, the great stimulant of life. Art as the only superior counter-force to all will to denial of life ...'[3]

Faith in art as a redemptive force in the anguished situation of modern humanity found its best-known expression in the Romantic movement. Romanticism, like all widespread cultural movements, is extremely hard to define or periodize in any neat and tidy way.

Like Hegelianism, the Romantic movement developed as a response to the one-sided rationalism of the eighteenth century, and against this rationalism the Romantics appealed to feeling, immediacy, and intuition as means of restoring the shattered unity of the human spirit. The Romantic outlook was eloquently expressed by the Norwegian philosopher Henrik Steffens, a disciple of Schelling, whose lectures in Copenhagen signalled the beginning of the Romantic movement in

Scandinavia. Steffens believed that humanity needed a holistic vision of truth, but, against Hegel, taught that this was not to be found through logic or dialectics, but through poetic intuition. The poet takes us into the ultimate sanctuary of truth where science may not tread. The poet, he held, communicates 'holy, radiant images of the eternal', 'no man, no age, is ever utterly bereft of a sense for such poetic revelations' in which

> a divine, a golden age, illuminated by an eternal sun, arises before our eyes, suddenly, as if by magic. An infinite meaning seems to be concealed behind every form and mystically shines out towards us. We are environed by an exalted and glorious radiance; a deep longing awakens in our inmost being, and irresistibly draws us towards this wonderful and magical world.[4]

Although this 'deep longing' often took the form of a profound nostalgia for a lost golden age, a heroic medieval or mythological past, many of the Romantics wanted to carry forward the Enlightenment's search for human freedom – only they wanted to do so in a new way. Instead of basing their humanism on a mechanistic science or on abstract moral axioms they believed that the true form of human freedom was to be found in the symbolic and imaginative world of art. Art is not opposed to reason, said Schelling, but the aesthetic intuition is the supreme expression of man's essential freedom and creativity. Art combines the polarities of human life which rationalism severely puts asunder: art is both conscious and unconscious; it is a 'work', something which the human being produces, and at the same time it is a grace, something which is inspired in him by a power which is more than the power of conscious decision. In aesthetic creation human work is no longer subjected to the production of impersonal, objectified commodities but to moulding and shaping forms which truly reflect our most intimate interests and concerns. In the work of art we do not contemplate a mere object – we see ourselves. Art is the mirror of the soul.

The Romantic conception of art and of the creative aesthetic imagination was vigorously expounded by Samuel Taylor Coleridge, who interpreted the doctrines of Schelling and the German Romantics to a (not altogether receptive) British audience. Coleridge summed up the Romantic teaching when he wrote of the poet that he

> brings the whole soul into activity, with the subordination of its faculties to each other according to their relative worth and dignity.

He diffuses a tone and spirit of unity, that blends, and (as it were) *fuses*, each into each, by that synthetic and magical power, to which I would exclusively appropriate the name of Imagination. This power ... reveals itself in the balance or reconcilement of opposite or discordant qualities: of sameness, with difference; of the general with the concrete; the idea with the image; the individual with the representative; the sense of novelty and freshness with old and familiar objects; a more than usual state of emotion with more than usual order; judgement ever awake and steady self-possession with enthusiasm and feeling profound or vehement; and while it blends and harmonizes the natural and the artificial, still subordinates art to nature; the manner to the matter; and our admiration for the poet to our sympathy with the poetry.[5]

In the eyes of the Romantics the poet was thus a figure who lived in a deep sympathy with the whole of the cosmic order and who, through his art, was able to transpose the conflicts and contradictions experienced in life into a harmonious and reconciling imaginative experience. This ideal of poetic reconciliation seemed to many to have found its ultimate expression in Goethe's *Faust*. Faust, the ambitious heaven-storming, hell-raising alchemist who sought to penetrate and to master nature's inmost secrets, but who only succeeds in bringing disaster on all those he loves, stood for the enquiring, doubting, dominating ethos of scientific and intellectual Enlightenment. In the final scene, however, Goethe (in contrast to other versions of the legend) has Faust being redeemed by the love of Margareta, the pure and innocent girl whom Faust had seduced and ruined. In this final scene Margareta is transfigured into a Beatrice-like heavenly figure who leads Faust to a vision of the divine glory, and the drama ends with a so-called 'mystical Chorus':

> All things corruptible are but a parable
> Earth's insufficiency here finds fulfilment
> Here the ineffable wins life through love
> The eternal feminine leads us on.

This ideal of ultimate reconciliation (even for the doubter Faust), a reconciliation which could most appropriately be expressed by means of (or embodied in) a work of art, superbly reflected the ideals of the Romantic generation. But the ideal was not merely something to be limited to the aesthetic media of stage or book or canvas. 'Poetry' for the Romantics was a way of life. In this respect it was Goethe's *Wilhelm Meister* which provided the paradigm. This novel – or rather this long, rambling, complex sequence of novels – depicted the tale of a young man in search of truth. The Romantics were not too happy about Goethe's rather practical and even mundane conclusions, but the idea of the quest itself, with its involved and often bizarre incidents, conspiracies and entertainments, provided a model for the poetic way of life. Not only in the case of *Wilhelm Meister* but with regard to the German *Bildungsroman* ('novel of education') tradition in general, the Romantics saw the individual search for the getting of wisdom as a key to the art of being human.

The Romantics' evaluation of aesthetic experience, and their intention to infuse a poetic spirit into life itself, has deeply permeated the structure of modern sensibility. Herbert Marcuse, for instance, defends the place of imagination in human life against the more crudely mechanistic forms of Marxism:

> The imagination, unifying sensibility and reason, becomes 'productive' as it becomes practical: a guiding force in the reconstruction of reality – a reconstruction with the help of a *gaya scienza*, a science and technology released from their service to destruction and exploitation, and thus free for the liberating exigencies of the imagination. The rational transformation of the world could then lead to a reality formed by the aesthetic sensibility of man. Such a world could (in a literal sense!) embody, incorporate the human faculties and desires to such an extent that they appear as part of the objective determinism of nature – coincidence of causality through nature and causality through freedom ... The aesthetic universe is the *Lebenswelt* on which the needs and faculties of freedom depend for their freedom.[6]

The theme of the *Bildungsroman* is thus transformed into a programme for society as a whole. As an anonymous wall-slogan put it during the Paris riots of 1968: 'L'imagination au pouvoir! – Power to the Imagination!'

The Romantic ideal has also made its presence felt in religion and theology. In fact, from its inception, Romanticism made quasi-religious claims on behalf of art, and rarely hesitated to use religious language and imagery in expounding its point of view. Recently theologians and philosophers of religion have been giving considerable attention to the role which imagination and aesthetic categories such as image, symbol and story might play in the religious consciousness. Many would agree with Mary Warnock that there is finally a convergence between the aesthetic and religious imagination, and that this aesthetic-religious imagination is – in opposition to Nietzsche – 'not merely the source of passing pleasures ... but of *truth*'.[7] The aesthetic intuition of a harmony 'deep down things' is, from this point of view, a real perception of the truth which lies at the heart of religion.

Kierkegaard had, to a certain extent, a natural sympathy with the Romantic vision, and in many ways he supported the Romantic protest against a too one-sided rationalism. In his journals he quoted approvingly from a commentary on Goethe's *Faust* which argued that only such an imaginative portrayal could make the idea of the Absolute 'living, effective and true', whereas a philosophical approach will always inevitably remain 'dry, dead and unenjoyable' (Pap. I C 97). Kierkegaard put this lesson into practice in many ways in his own work, so that even his most philosophically precise works are presented in a startlingly lively and even poetic manner, with brilliant images and stories woven into the tight conceptual structure of the philosophical argument. In fact it is extremely difficult to differentiate between 'philosophy' and 'literature' in many of his works, several of which could be read as novels in the *Bildungsroman* tradition. Moreover, he had a serious and abiding appreciation of the 'aesthetic universe' and his writings contain frequent discussions of music, literature and theatre as well as of aesthetic theory.

Following the Romantics, Kierkegaard saw the perfect work of art as reflecting a unitary, harmonious vision of reality in which differences and oppositions were reconciled by the invisible threads which bound everything into a single whole. Like the Romantics he regarded *Wilhelm Meister* as an outstanding example of such an aesthetic achievement. The novel, he wrote, 'is truly the whole world seen in a mirror, a true microcosm' (JP 1455). His susceptibility to imaginative experience is attested throughout his work. The way in which such experience affected him is eloquently expressed in the following journal entry:

> When I am weary of everything and 'full of days' fairy tales are always a refreshing, renewing bath for me. *There* all earthly, finite cares vanish; joy, yes, even sorrow are infinite ... one completely forgets the particular, private sorrows which every man can have, in order to plunge into the deep-seated sorrow common to all ... (JP 5287)

We can see from this that Kierkegaard regarded the reconciling power of art and of imagination as independent of whether or not the work has a 'happy ending'. What it depends on is the very form of imagination as such, even when the poetic theme is that of 'deep-seated sorrow'. Commenting on Lessing's discussion of Aristotle's theory of the cathartic function of 'fear and pity' in tragedy, Kierkegaard suggests that these tragic passions work by drawing us out of ourselves in contemplation of the tragic portrayal of suffering enacted before us (SLW, pp. 454–65; cf. JP 4826). Such a tragic catharsis is essentially as purifying and as reconciling as anything achieved by a happy ending. It is the aesthetic form, the imaginative experience itself which simply as such possesses a unifying and harmonizing power.

But although Kierkegaard's view of the imagination and of art is largely drawn within the horizon set by Romanticism his judgement concerning the ultimate validity of such aesthetic experience is radically different. For he argues that the reconciliation brought about by art is ultimately illusory. The gulf between aesthetic experience and the way things are in the real world is made clear in the following entry from the journals; an entry which begins by describing a kind of day-dream experience which he regards as fundamentally akin to aesthetic experience:

> One dozes, as it were, in the totality of things (a pantheistic element, without producing strength as does the religious) in an oriental reverie in the infinite, in which everything appears to be fiction – and one is reconciled as in a grand poem: the being of the whole world, the being of God, and my own being are poetry in which all the multiplicity, the wretched disparities of life ... are reconciled in a misty, dreamy existence. But then, regrettably, I wake up again, and the very same tragic relativity in everything begins worse than ever ... (JP 1019)

Art is illusion, dream, fiction; it is the power of wish-fulfilment mastering the reality-principle. Art does not really solve humanity's conflict with the world and with itself, but by virtue of the act of imaginative representation it lifts both the creator and the recipient of the work out of the agonized immediacy of this conflict. Even when art represents the most horrific conflicts the fact that we are dealing with art, with imagination, and not directly with reality means that the horror is experienced at one remove. Art is thus in some measure at least in conflict with truth. None the less, our capacity for such experience is part of our essential humanity: Kierkegaard's own enthusiasm for the arts, and above all for the theatre, being evidenced on page after page of his writings. 'There is no young person with any imagination', he wrote, 'who has not at least once felt themselves caught in the magical world of the theatre and longed to be themselves carried away into that artificial reality ...' (FT/R, p. 154). Such an experience is intrinsically healthy. In falling under the spell of what Kierkegaard calls the 'shadow-figures' of the theatrical repertoire a young person gains a kind of insight into their own possibilities. By projecting themselves into and identifying themselves with the fictive personae of the stage, young people learn to know their own capacity for grief, rage, jealousy, romantic feeling, love, self-sacrifice, nobility, etc. It is in a sense a young person's right to play with such possibilities, to 'try on' the different roles in imagination. But at the same time we must learn to distinguish between the realm of aesthetic illusion and the real world. Unless we do this the personality simply evaporates in the boundless miasma of pure imagination. Writing of the theatrical shadow-world, Kierkegaard speaks of a moment when 'the cock crows, and the shadow figures flee away as the voices of the night fall silent. If they continue, then we are in a quite different territory, where everything occurs under the disturbing gaze of [ethical] responsibility, then we are close to the demonic' (FT/R, p. 156). The world of imagination is a world of dreams and to live healthily we must be able to dream but we must also be able to distinguish between dreams and reality. It is one thing for a young person to picture themselves as a Don Juan, a Faust or a Master Thief – it is quite another matter if they try to live out such an 'image' in real life.

In *Stages on Life's Way* Kierkegaard portrays a group of aesthetic personalities who fail to make this vital distinction and who try to live their lives on aesthetic principles. They devise a sumptuous nocturnal banquet in a lonely hunting lodge some miles from the city at which they make eloquent speeches on the theme of love. In Kierkegaard's description of the banquet the revellers assume magnificent and almost supernatural dimensions. But when dawn breaks the feast ends and we see them pacing up and down a country lane, waiting for a change of horses to take them back to the city. Now they make quite a different impression, which, Kierkegaard tells us, is 'almost uncanny'.

One might think of ghosts overtaken by the dawn; of subterranean creatures which cannot find the crack through which they vanish because it is only visible in the dark; of unfortunates for whom the difference between day and night has vanished in their suffering's monotony. (SLW, p. 82)

Here Kierkegaard gives flesh to the failure to distinguish between what is proper to the realm of art and what belongs to the realm of moral responsibility. To put it simply: when we leave the theatre we have to renounce the innocent conjuring with the myriad of fictive possibilities and choose for ourselves a place and course in life.

Kierkegaard's first major work, *Either-Or*, spells out at length the implications of this moment of decision. The first volume of this two-volume work contains a collection of aphorisms, essays, reviews and, finally, a short novel, *The Seducer's Diary*. These combine to present the aesthetic attitude. The Seducer is the supreme embodiment of this attitude: not satisfied with aesthetic experience confined to its proper sphere (in the theatre, in literature, etc.), he tries to *live* aesthetically and to this end uses a series of erotic encounters as a way of experiencing in life the sort of pleasures which others find in art; his existence is the acting out of a self-cast role – 'the Seducer'. Despite this awesome title, the Seducer is in fact a pitiable creature. His relationships with his 'victims' are, in the strict sense of the word, merely occasional – that is, he uses them as occasions, as means to gratify his own fantasies. He is incapable of a real meeting, a real encounter with another person, incapable of dealing with a situation of mutual responsibility. He is a perpetual adolescent whose contact with the solid world of bourgeois life is at best tangential. Locked up in his own dream-world he slips silently through the real world like a shadow moving across the floor (EO 1, pp. 9, 306, 310). Although Kierkegaard uses the Seducer to exemplify a viciously aesthetic attitude, we should not be misled into thinking that the essence of his depravity lies in the sexual nature of his activities. The key issue is the confusion between art and life. In this sense Kierkegaard could equally have used, for example, the General, the Great Actor, the Hero, the Inventor, the Discoverer, the Saint, etc. What he is showing is what happens when one tries to base life on an 'image'.

The second volume of *Either-Or* represents quite a different attitude, which Kierkegaard calls the ethical. This attitude is represented by a bourgeois civil servant, a married man with responsibilities and commitments in the real social world. In two lengthy letters he exhorts a youthful and aesthetically minded friend to snap out of it, to grow up and come to terms with real life. Finally, he sends the text of a sermon delivered by a friend of his who has become a parson in the lonely heathland of Jutland, where the 'eye discovers not a soul' and a man is alone with God (EO 2, p. 338). We never find out what becomes of the young man, for *Either-Or* is not a story in that sense but the presentation of two conflicting points of view, two attitudes to life, and it is designed to illuminate a fundamental decision each of us has at some point and in some way to make. It is a decision which determines whether we achieve selfhood in the full sense or merely remain in the fantastic half-light of the aesthetic universe.

The failure to transcend the aesthetic stage of life is connected by Kierkegaard with the whole question of suffering and its place in human life. Art, he seems to say, is somehow tied up with our response to what Nietzsche was to call the *Urschmerz*, the sheer agony of existence with which we are confronted when we live at the level of primitivity. Art is one way of beautifying, transfiguring and so concealing the basic, irreconcilable conflict between man and the world, between man's aspiration to live a free, spiritually determined life and the omnipresent constraints of physicality. In the face of this conflict the aesthetic point of view is a proclamation of peace where there is no peace. In what is one of his most powerful images, Kierkegaard recalls the story of the tyrant Phalaris who had a brazen bull fashioned for him in which he roasted his enemies alive. He had the bull made in such a way that the cries of the victims were modulated into music by a system of carefully contrived pipes. Here is how Kierkegaard uses the story:

> What is a poet? An unhappy man who conceals deep pains in his heart, but whose lips are so fashioned that when the sigh and the cry pass out of them they sound like beautiful music. His situation is like that of the unfortunate person who was slowly tortured by a soft flame in the Ox of Phalaris, whose screams could not reach that tyrant and so affright him because he heard them as sweet music. (EO 1, p. 19)

Aesthetic creativity is thus seen by Kierkegaard as dependent on a profound inner alienation. Far from testifying to the healing of man's divided self, art is rather an eternal witness to the radical seriousness of this split – which means that we have to interpret art as a phenomenon very cautiously. One might draw an analogy here to the way in which psycho-analysis interprets a patient's dreams, finding in them a content which is not merely different from, but which actually contradicts the patient's conscious intentions: in the same way the real message of art is virtually the opposite of the message which the artist, or at least his

Romantic apologist, thinks he has put in it. The artist is, in a phrase from Kierkegaard's journals, 'an unconscious sacrifice' (JP 1027), for he does not comprehend the source or significance of the suffering by which his creative work is in fact fuelled.

None the less, Kierkegaard believes, in the modern age, the age of reflection, art comes closer and closer towards revealing its own limitations and its fundamental questionableness. Alongside the optimistic, harmonious vision of art expounded by thinkers such as Schelling and Steffens there was also a strongly dualistic streak in Romanticism, which could easily lead to a preoccupation with themes of discord and despair. In a figure such as Coleridge it is perhaps not hard to see these two conflicting tendencies brought together in a single individual. This struggle between poetic optimism and intellectual doubt as to the power of art to conquer all is most vividly portrayed in his 'Dejection: An Ode'. In this poem Coleridge conjures up a sombre impression of

> A grief without a pang, void, dark and drear,
> A stifled, drowsy, unimpassioned grief,
> Which finds no natural outlet, no relief,
> In word, or sigh, or tear.

Coleridge himself regards this mood as a result of the springs of his 'shaping Spirit of Imagination' – a force which he variously describes as 'strong music in the soul', a 'fair, luminous mist', 'a beautiful and beauty-making power' – drying up. Many commentators take this analysis at its face value; Kierkegaard, however, would turn it round: in his view it is the dejection, the despair, which is the prime mover in the aesthetic sphere – it is this which sets the imagination to work in the first place. The 'luminous mist' of imagination is woven by the artist to conceal the 'sightless and drear' chasm (Shelley) which lurks in the recesses of his soul: it is a way of evading his ownmost truth. The evaporation of the aesthetic mist compels him to confront the blank abyss within. In 'dejection' the poet at last, unwillingly and still not entirely honestly, sees of what stuff he is made.

If the nihilistic element in Romanticism only emerged in a veiled form in the first generation of Romantic writers, it became much more explicit in the following decades, as poets like Byron, Shelley and Heinrich Heine held out words and images of revolt and despair to a generation which was ready to receive them. In Novalis' novel *Heinrich von Ofterdingen* (one of the paradigmatic works of early Romanticism) the journey through life is depicted as leading 'ever homeward', and for Schelling the whole of history can be represented as a great Odyssey of the spirit, as our eternal homecoming. But for the younger generation, the generation which directly influenced Kierkegaard himself, the path through life was a path into the unknown and unknowable, 'the most desolate' way, leading beyond heaven and hell, beyond good and evil, ready to face without illusions the amoral nature of the universe.

Why does the just man drag himself
Bloody and suffering beneath the weight of the cross
While joyous as a victor
The wicked man trots by on a noble steed?

Who is guilty? Is perhaps
Our Lord not quite so powerful?
Or does he himself perpetrate these crimes?
Oh, that would be contemptible.

So we go on asking
Till, with a handful of earth,
Our mouths are finally stopped –
But is that an answer?[8]

Kierkegaard saw this shift from optimism to pessimism as part of a clear dialectical pattern running through the whole development of modern poetry and art, a pattern he saw exemplified in the archetypal figures of Don Juan, Faust and the Wandering Jew. He saw these figures as representing the three great forms of life outside religion, namely, sensuous passion, doubt and nihilistic despair. They thus stood for the major themes of profane post-renaissance art and, for Kierkegaard, were concretely embodied in Mozart's Don Giovanni, Goethe's Faust and the nihilistic themes of Romantic pessimism. The 'dialectical' aspect of the relationship between these three figures is that they respectively articulate a higher degree of self-consciousness: in Don Juan feeling is everything, and the almost naively amorous knight has no real understanding of his predicament until the very closing moments of the drama when, of course, it is too late; Faust, however, is aware of the step he is taking in conjuring up Mephistopheles, thereby deliberately setting aside the injunctions of revealed religion – although he still remains susceptible to the pull of human feelings, and has, however distorted, a kind of aspiration to nobility; over against Faust, the Wandering Jew (a mythical figure of medieval legend, condemned to an earthly immortality for cursing Christ) is inescapably aware of his own perdition as he wanders the earth indifferent to the affairs of those around him, longing only for extinction, for the cessation of this unending death in life. Both Kierkegaard and his beloved teacher, Poul Martin Møller, were fascinated by the symbolic figure of the Wandering Jew, and Møller wrote a series of aphorisms, *Ahasverus*, which expressed the mood of utter world-weariness which Ahasverus represented. In one of these aphorisms he has Ahasverus declare: 'Your ignorant priests believe that there is an absolute difference between good and evil, but they do not observe that I stand precisely at the zero-point on life's thermometer.'[9] It is this 'zero-point' which Kierkegaard saw coming to expression in the aesthetic nihilism of his generation.

In the first part of *Either-Or* we encounter an aesthetic society or club who call themselves 'The Symparanekromenoi', an invented Greek title which can loosely be translated as the 'fellowship of buried lives'. The outlook of this society embodies the standpoint of just such self-conscious aesthetic nihilism. Here their philosophy is summed up in a speech made at one of their nocturnal gatherings:

> Men may well assert that God's voice is not in the raging storm but in the gentle breeze; but our ears are not shaped to hear gentle breezes, but rather to devour the roar of the elements. And why should it not break forth more violently still and make an end to life and to the world and to this short address, which at least has the advantage over other things that it soon comes to an end. Yes, let that vortex which is the innermost principle of the world ... break forth and with vehement wrathfulness bring down the mountains, nations, creations of culture and mankind's clever achievements, let it break forth with the last dreadful shriek which, more surely than the final trumpet, will signal the downfall of all things ... (EO 1, p. 168)

In this nihilistic perspective art comes to express ever more clearly its own inability to supply a religiously durable solution to the crisis of human existence. Art is merely a 'painted veil' cast over a chaotic 'wild vortex'.

Following once more in Møller's footsteps, Kierkegaard regarded the pessimism of the literary 'left' as a bitter fruit of the cult of irony in the first, superficially optimistic, wave of Romanticism. The concept of irony did indeed play a key role in early Romanticism, and it was used by the Romantic theorists to justify their claims for the playfully creative freedom of the poet, and his elevation above the customs and standards of conventional society, both in art and life. The ironic attitude was one in which the whole of the phenomenal world, the world of appearances, was seen as no more than a product of the creative imagination. All outward forms were, from the standpoint of irony, indifferent as regards their essential content: all that really mattered was the poetic spirit which gave them meaning and shape. In this way the poet was as much entitled to use the grotesque, the morbid or the ugly as a vehicle for his ideas as the traditional ideals of beauty which had inspired 'classical' art. The Romantic poet was as much at home with chaos and disorder as with the measured forms of a more orderly beauty. Thus the 'Romantic' book could, and in theory should, combine an apparently limitless array of literary genres: narrative, lyrical poetry, aphorisms, essays, etc. For the point was that external form was regarded as merely relative and secondary, while it was the 'idea' alone which truly mattered.

Kierkegaard saw in this doctrine of irony a dangerous separation of subject and object, of idea and form, of selfhood and substance. He refused to believe that the human imagination was absolutely creative in the way that the Romantics seemed to assert it was. As we have already seen in discussing his view of Socratic irony, irony for Kierkegaard cannot by itself produce or create anything but can only criticize, question or confound. It follows that if someone tries to make irony into their supreme or even their sole value their world will lose all solidity and continuity and experience will dissolve into a sequence of wildly capricious moods. The ironist eventually becomes the creature rather than the creator of these moods and incapable of the resolve needed to break through to a religiously grounded ethical life. Referring to one of the best-known Romantic 'cult' novels Kierkegaard comments wryly that the Romantics were only too right in their idealization of the *Taugenichts* ('good-for-nothing') since 'nothing' is precisely the state to which the Romantic philosophy leads (CI, p. 281).

This becomes clear in the second, nihilistic wave of Romanticism.

In *Stages on Life's Way* Kierkegaard powerfully (if laboriously) evokes this Romantic destiny by means of the central character of the second half of this (once more two-part) book. This character, who has no name and is known to us solely as 'Quidam', 'a certain one', describes his personal descent into the void in a long and complex diary.

There is nothing new under the sun, says Solomon. Well, be that as it may it is worse when nothing at all happens ... Of course, if my pain were rich in incident, with changes of scenery and decor then it would have some interest. But my suffering is boring. It is true: I am still continually expressing this nothing and the scene is the same without any alteration. (SLW, pp. 346–7)

The diary concludes with the poignant lines:

The diary ends here for now. It deals with nothing ... It contains nothing, but if, as Cicero says, the easiest letter is that which deals with nothing, yet it is sometimes the heaviest life which deals with nothing. (SLW, p. 397)

In the diary we are shown that Quidam's journey into nothingness is the result of having made his almost hyperactive imagination the determining element in his personality. His melancholy is rooted in the fact that he has allowed imagination to be a substitute for life. By means of this 'Quidam' Kierkegaard gives us a concrete image of where the Romantic principle must, in the end, lead us.

It would not be hard to find a great deal of supporting evidence for Kierkegaard's claim that art in the modern age is impelled to become more and more explicitly nihilistic. The attack on traditional canons of beauty, harmony and order seems to have become still more radical with each generation that has passed since his time. Writing of the murals painted by the abstract expressionist painter Mark Rothko in the chapel of Rice University, Houston, Robert Hughes has written: 'Subjectless, formless ... and almost without internal relationships ... they represent an astonishing degree of self-banishment. All the world has drained out of them, leaving only a void ... In effect, the Rothko Chapel is the last silence of Romanticism.'[10]

The same story is repeated in the other arts. With regard to music, Gerald Abraham speaks of the musical scene of the early twentieth century as reflecting 'a sense that the great tradition was approaching a dead end', and adds that

While the Western tradition emerged thus cracked and enfeebled after the Second War, the process of fragmentation soon went much deeper and resulted in wide open breaks. *Musique Concrète* and electrophonic music opened up exploration of an art of pure sound completely lacking in the associations normal music had imperceptibly acquired during the centuries, and therefore devoid of meaning and incapable of communication.[11]

In the face of such internal crises the Romantic claim that it is art and the aesthetic intuition which corresponds to it that will save us from the 'desolation row' of rationalism sounds increasingly hollow. Far from acting as a bulwark against nihilism, art itself, as Hans Küng has said, is seen today 'against a nihilistic background', and, just as philosophers and theologians have spoken of the 'death of God', so artists and art critics have mooted the 'death of art'.[12] Nor has postmodernism yet achieved more than to give a further twist to the knife.

We tend to think of this situation as very much a twentieth-century phenomenon but, as we have seen, Kierkegaard was already alive to the tendencies that have moulded our contemporary aesthetic situation. In fact even before Kierkegaard's time Hegel had argued that art had been relativized by the rationality of modernity. 'The peculiar nature of artistic production and of works of art', he had written, 'no longer fills our highest need ... Thought and reflection have spread their wings above fine art.' 'Art, considered in its highest vocation, is and remains for us a thing of the past.' Much as we may be moved by art – and Hegel himself was very receptive to art – we no longer give to it the quasi-religious reverence which it had at certain times in the past come to evoke: 'no matter how excellent we find the statues of the greek gods, no matter how we see God the Father, the Christ and Mary so estimably and perfectly portrayed: it is no help; we bow the knee no longer'.[13]

Hegel's critique of art offers a useful contrast to that of Kierkegaard. In Hegel's view, the essential point was that art, religion and philosophy all function as forms of the Absolute. Each of these forms expresses the same ultimate content, but they do so in different ways. Art, because it deals in sensuous imagery and is thus tied to the forms of the external world, is the least adequate of these three forms, since it is inherently incapable of reflecting the purely spiritual essence of the Absolute. The parabolic nature of art has had a valuable educational role in the history of human consciousness, but we have now, in Hegel's view, reached a point where we can know the Absolute 'face to face'. We no longer need an external image to guide reason into the inner sanctuary of reason's own truth. Hegel thus sees the history of art as involving a progressive refinement of form such that in each succeeding period of history art works more spiritually. Thus the subject matter of art shifts from the grotesque animal deities of ancient Egypt to the beautifully anthropomorphic divinities of Greek sculpture to the purely humanistic themes of modern art. In each epoch art expresses more and more clearly the truth that the real subject matter of art, the real subject (in both senses!) of art is humanity in its free spiritual creativity. But although art comes to the point of revealing humanity to itself as the true focus of meaning in the world, it cannot itself explain or interpret the real dynamics of human existence. It can show us to ourselves; it cannot explain us to ourselves. This is the task reserved for philosophy – in the sense expounded in the preceding chapter. Art, in the last resort, fails to meet the modern demand for absolute self-transparency and objectivity.

Kierkegaard did not dispute that ultimately art is humanistic. Where he disagreed with Hegel was concerning the continuity between art, religion and philosophy. He did not accept that these all had the same essential content. The content of religion, at least, is radically, qualitatively different from the content of either art or philosophy, and the difference is not merely one of form but of substance. In acquiring a consciousness of its own fundamental humanism, art does not, in his view, thereby express the 'same' truth as that with which religion is concerned. On the contrary, the more humanistic, the more profane, the more secular art becomes, the more it will be led to testify to its own nullity and to the fact that religion is essentially alien to it. One can only speak of modern art as 'religious' in the negative sense that it ruthlessly and honestly strips away man's pretensions to absoluteness. It is in this sense that Paul Tillich speaks of expressionist art as revealing man's finitude and alienation from God and thus as preparing the way for the religious consciousness.[14] Don Cupitt makes a similar point with regard to Piet Mondrian:

> ... the best abstract paintings by him and others have often been seen as icons of religious minimalism. They express a deep conviction that in the twentieth century, and indeed for the foreseeable future, we need to find out how light we can travel; we need to learn a kind of Buddhist inner simplicity and even emptiness.[15]

Modern art strips away the baroque encrustations from the altars of the faith. But to argue for such an indirect witness by art to the religious search – something one could do on the basis of Kierkegaard's view of the progress of modern art – is very different from what Hegel is trying to say. Hegel says that art expresses the truth and that it is only its form which is inadequate. Kierkegaard and other religious existentialists assert that the utmost art can do is to tell us that we do not possess the truth, while it is precisely the profane, humanistic core of art which prevents it from speaking the transcendent word that sets us free.

For Kierkegaard as for Hegel art meets its match in the reflective, rational, objective character of the modern age. The shrewd bourgeois spirit of the present age vitiates the vital passion, the 'immediacy', on which great art depends. 'The age of poetry thus seems to be over', he writes, 'and especially tragedy.' And, he adds, 'a comic poet will lack a public, for not even the public can be in two places at once – in its seats and in the play' (SLW, p. 412).

The link between the crisis of art and the character of the present age is underlined by the fact that Kierkegaard's most sustained analysis of this present age occurs in the context of one of his literary reviews. This is a book-length discussion of a relatively minor novel called *Two Ages*, which contrasts the age of the French Revolution with the present bourgeois age. Kierkegaard uses this originally literary discussion as the jumping-off point for a full examination of 'the present age'. It will therefore be appropriate to conclude this chapter by looking at this 'review'.

As we have already seen, Kierkegaard believed that the essential nature of aesthetic experience is to be found in its power to give a sense of harmony, unity and reconciliation in place of the harsh dissonances and conflicts with which life confronts us. He drew a distinction, however, between those writers who were 'poets' in a derogatory sense, writers whose work was nothing but the projection of fantastic, unrealized and unrealizable dreams, and those 'authors' whose work reflected a solid 'life-view' which they had in fact achieved for themselves in life. Such a life-view is (in Schweitzer's sense) the expression of a profound ethical optimism. It may not be the driving-force which motivates the martyr or the saint, but it works

> ... by understanding how to find a milder aspect in which to see suffering, by having the patience which expects good fortune to smile again, by the friendly sympathy of caring people, by the resignation which does not renounce everything but only the highest, and by the contentment that changes the second best into something just as good as the highest ... (TA, p. 19)

This life-view represents a consciously maintained reconciliation of sense and reason, experience and idealism, society and the individual. But what Kierkegaard finds most interesting in the contrast which the novel draws between the 'two ages' of the title is that it raises the question as to how far such a life-view can be achieved under the conditions of life in the present age of reflection and doubt. 'The quiet joy over life' which is the fruit of the life-view is scorned by the sceptics of the radical left and inaccessible to the busy bustling bourgeoisie with its myriad of worldly concerns. The present age has no use for continuity but constantly demands newness – 'The momentary, a brilliant beginning, and a new era dating from this are the little that is understood' (TA, p. 10).

Out of concern for oneself to allow oneself to be guided, inwardly and admiringly to be able to delight in the achievement of the older person who has remained true to himself, to be edified by the spectacle of fifty years' faithful service, to understand slowly, to learn from the person of honour, from whom one learns something quite different than from the personalities of the moment – no one seems to have the patience to learn what it is to be human and to renounce the inhuman in this way. (TA, p. 11)

The bourgeois revolution snaps the threads of continuity with tradition which are essential if humanity is to have a hopeful, harmonious life-view – and, Kierkegaard believes, it is just such a life-view which is necessary if we are to have an art which can truly feed our ethical and religious needs. Art can only nourish the ethical self when it is itself based on a firmly held ethical position – but it is precisely the character of the modern age that it destroys the presuppositions of such a position, with the result that art itself inevitably withers in the barren fields of 'the nineteenth-century rational man'. By setting his phenomenology of the present 'rational, reflecting, unimpassioned age' in the context of the review, Kierkegaard is plainly saying that far from art being a redemptive force, it is the destiny of art too to fall victim to the dialectics of modernity, as publicity takes the place of action, spectating the place of participation, money of passion, envy of enthusiasm, levelling of nobility and greatness, meetings and ballots of leadership, the public of community, idle chatter of serious conversation (and serious listening). The pursuit of modernism in art is thus unwittingly a kind of aesthetic suicide, perhaps most concretely symbolized in the brief vogue for 'auto-destructive art' in the 1960s. Profane art cannot of itself do more than to lay bare the nothingness which lies coiled at the heart of human life. If art is to achieve more than this it can only do so by sinking roots into a dimension of life that is more than aesthetic. Art, Kierkegaard maintains, provides no ultimate refuge for the human spirit. There is no golden city at the end of the rainbow bridge – only the yawning abyss of inescapable nothingness. It is culpable to linger too long in the magical twilight of the theatre when the business of the day confronts us with passionate urgency, and to place one's hopes upon the aesthetic universe is, in the present age, to evade the full force of the challenge which nihilism has posed for us.

By means of the critique of philosophy and science on the one hand and the critique of art on the other, Kierkegaard has thus ruled out the two main forms of the theoretical life as possible 'answers' to the question of modern existence. We have frequently observed that over against these theoretical forms he sets the exigencies of what he calls the 'ethical' or 'religious' life, and we now have to look more closely at what this means.

SIX

BECOMING AN INDIVIDUAL

WHEN WE TURN from Kierkegaard's critique of what he regarded as the various false 'cures' for healing the sickness of the modern age to his account of the radical therapy offered by the way of authentic religion, we should not expect to find any clear-cut description of the promised land that lies beyond the wasteland of modern nihilism. His concern is not to tell us what the Christian life consists of in terms of a set of beliefs and practices, but to tease out how it is that one becomes a Christian. 'Objectivity emphasizes "what" is said; subjectivity emphasizes "how" it is said ... Objectivity only asks about the forms of thought, subjectivity asks about inwardness. At its maximum this "how" is the passion of infinity, and the passion of infinity is itself truth' (CUP 1, pp. 202–3). To give a description of the Christian life or of the reward one might receive for following that life, to describe the God who is the object of faith – all this would be to fall into the trap of objectifying religion, a mistake which Kierkegaard regards contemporary religion as having made! If religion is really to provide an alternative to the spirit of the age it must start by refusing to accept the agenda set by the world. Religion can operate effectively only if it does so on its own terms. Once one tries to explain religion 'objectively' in order to win over the cultured despisers, one makes it impossible to bring out the real issue with which religion confronts us because one has moved out of the sphere of subjectivity in which alone religious truth is true. Subjectivity is the 'how' of religious faith. But it is more than that because for Kierkegaard there is an intrinsic connection between ends and means. As far as religion is concerned, to have grasped the 'how' is also to have grasped the 'what'; to exist subjectively is not just the way by which to discover religious truth but is itself to exist religiously, to live 'in truth'.

> ... one thinks that the end is the main thing; one requires that the one who is striving should reach the end without being too precisely concerned about the means. But this is not so, and to reach the end in this way is ungodly impatience. In the sight of eternity the relationship between means and ends is rather the opposite. (UDVS, p. 141)

In relation to eternity the means are every bit as important as the end. It is not as if eternal life were some kind of reward bestowed in a purely external way on those who had earned it here below: it is rather being in a right relation to eternity, it is an internal quality of the religious life. God cannot be the end of all our striving unless we are prepared to strive in a godly manner.

Here we can see another element in Kierkegaard's strategy of indirect communication. If subjectivity is an essential quality of the religious life then the communication of religious truth must itself be carried out in such a way as to stimulate and awaken the subjectivity of both participants in the communication process. The communication cannot just present the reader or recipient with a ready-made 'objective' solution: it must confront us with a choice and give us the responsibility for deciding what to do with it, to accept it or reject it. Therefore, as the actual author of his pseudonymous books, Kierkegaard disappears behind the masks of the various pseudonyms so that we have to decide for ourselves what is the right response to the books. We cannot take the short-cut of finding out what Kierkegaard the author actually thinks and allowing ourselves to be dictated to by that: it is as if the pseudonymous authorship were a kind of massive detective story of the 'whodunit' variety – only there is no final scene in which all is revealed; rather we have to make up our own minds and judge for ourselves. Readers are alone with the text without the authority of the author to guide their reading. Thus the act of reading itself involves risk and decision: to be committed to an interpretation of the text is already to have made a beginning in the way of ethical existence and subjectivity. For in the case of these texts what is at stake is not just what we might believe Kierkegaard qua author to have intended but what are to count as the ultimate values by which we direct and orientate our lives.

This conforms to Kierkegaard's view that subjectivity means responsibility and responsibility means individuality. The crowd is untruth because it is a way of refusing moral responsibility; truth depends totally on the emergence of individuals who are willing to take responsibility for their own lives, without, or even against, the guidance of the spirit of the age.

> For me ... this thing about the individual is the most decisive thing ... 'The individual' is the category through which, from a religious point of view, the age, history, the race must go ... My task is ... if possible to occasion, to invite, to move the many to force their way through this narrow pass, 'the individual', through which, note well,

no one can go without becoming themselves 'the individual' . . . 'The individual' is, Christianly speaking, the decisive category, and will also become decisive for the future of Christianity. (PV, pp. 124, 130–1, 135)

Only as individuals can we live subjectively, primitively, existentially, ethically, religiously, and in a sense all these terms point to the one personal reality. It should be clear that the individual in this sense is quite a different creature from the individual beloved of contemporary right-wing politicians for whom individualism is a matter of rights relating to property, money and time. Freedom of choice as a political slogan is the ideology of precisely that social order which Kierkegaard saw as obliterating the true primitive depths of genuine individuality. In Kierkegaard's view, becoming a religious individual is a matter of inwardness, of conscience, a step 'which even the prisoner, who is not free to move, even the man in chains, whose foot is not free can still take' (UDVS, p. 104). But how to take that step?

The Unrecognizability of God

We have seen how Kierkegaard regarded 'the present age' as an age in which the self-deification of the establishment, the idolatry of the masses, and the debasing of humanity to 'the numerical' brought about a complete effacing of the significance of the individual. Similarly the one-dimensional discourses of science and journalism drain language itself of the means by which to utilize the basic words which in the past served to carry and to express the religious tradition. This is the situation of a world of institutionalized unbelief, a world which, even when it uses the language, symbols, rites and ceremonies of the religious tradition, is no longer in touch with authentic religion. It is an age which is 'without God in the world'. In such an age there can be no question of a direct and unambiguous relation to God. For God is

so unnoticeable, so secretly present in His handiwork, that it could well happen that a man could live his life, get married, be noticed and respected as a man, a father, head of the shoot, without discovering God's presence in His handiwork, without ever once really getting any impression of the infinity of the ethical life . . . (CUP I, p. 244)

– and this is just as true if the person in question is also religious, taking part in the religious observances of wherever they happen to live.

Kierkegaard does not, of course, regard the concealment of God in creation as something new, as if God had at a certain point in history decided to withdraw from the scene and leave the world to its own devices. It is not just the modern age that is denied a direct relationship with him. The opacity of creation in relation to the creator is intrinsic to its character as creation. None the less, the modern age does experience the absence of God in a particularly sharp way. In paganism, Kierkegaard suggests, the gods were conceived of in naturalistic categories such that they were immediately recognizable for what they were. 'All paganism consists in this, that God relates himself directly to man as that which causes amazement to the wondering observer' (CUP 1, p. 245). The pagan consciousness is moved to worship by sudden, overwhelmingly beautiful or overwhelmingly terrifying appearances: the lightning-blast, the wind, the sea, the extraordinarily large or powerful, an uncanny natural formation, a man-shaped rock or tree. It is in such sublime experiences that paganism recognizes the divine. In this sense 'modern man' is also essentially pagan:

... therefore if God were to give Himself the form of a rare and monstrously large green bird with a red beak sitting in a tree on the hill, and perhaps even singing in a way never heard before: then the society man would take notice ... (CUP 1, p. 245)

Over against this pagan outlook Christianity has, historically, acted as a demythologizing force. But even within Christianity the divine was for a long time conceived of as standing in a merely relative relation to the world in such a way that particular institutions, places or people could be believed to possess a peculiar divine quality. Kierkegaard sees this as the essential standpoint of the Middle Ages, particularly in the way that the cloister became a tangible symbol of religiousness and in the measuring of Christian progress in terms of the external distinctions embodied in the spiritual and political hierarchy of the Church. In the modern age, however, the power of the traditional symbols has been drained by the Reformation and the Enlightenment. The outward forms of religion are no longer experienced as expressing real inward truth. A radical disjunction between symbol and meaning has cut into the typical modern consciousness. Neither for belief nor for unbelief is any immediate, direct relationship to God still viable. There is no unambiguous word, deed, institution or symbol which can be said to be inalienably expressive of supernatural authority. In this situation the believer will be undistinguishable in the crowd. There will be no aura, no quasi-sensuous 'presence' to mark him out. This is powerfully expressed by Kierkegaard in the renowned description of the 'knight of faith'.

> Here he is. Introductions being made I am presented to him. In the very moment when I clap eyes on him I push him away and myself take a leap backwards, clapping my hands together and saying half aloud: 'My God! Is this the man, is it really him, why he looks just like a tax collector!' Yet he is the one. I draw a little closer to him, observing his slightest movements, in case a little heterogenous telegraph signal from infinity should show itself, a glance, an expression, a gesture, a melancholy, a smile, betraying the infinite in its heterogeneity from the finite. No! I examine his figure from top to toe, in case there should be a crack through which the infinite peeped out. No! He is solid right through ... he totally belongs in this world, no bourgeois philistine more so. There is nothing to discover in this strange and noble being by which one could recognize him as the knight of infinity. (FT/R, pp. 38–9)

Religious existence in the modern world must be rooted in such 'hidden inwardness', and religious authority will no longer be invested in publicly recognizable hierarchies but will be exercised by those who 'will be unrecognizable like plain-clothes policemen, whose respective badges of office are hidden from view' (TA, p. 107).

> And none of the unrecognizable ones will dare vouch for himself by helping directly, speaking directly, teaching directly, making decisions at the head of the crowd ... This would get him dismissed, because he would be dabbling in the short-sighted ingenuity of human sympathy instead of obeying divine orders ... (TA, p. 98)

This throws further light on what can be seen as a positive aspect to the levelling process, even if the agents of levelling are themselves regarded as wrongly motivated. For in the wake of levelling no one can lean on the authority or the intercession of another but each and every one who comes to God must do so under their own flag, as individuals.

> '... see, the sharp scythe of levelling allows all, each for himself, to leap over the blade – see, God is waiting! Leap, then, into God's arms.' But even if it were the most trusted of the unrecognizable

ones, and even if it were the girl ... for whom he would offer up his life, he must not dare to help, for each person must make the leap him or herself, and God's infinite love must not become a second-hand relationship. (TA, pp. 108–9)

Perhaps then Kierkegaard's view of levelling contains something like Hegel's notion of the 'cunning of history', whereby (in Hegel's view) reason is able to turn to advantage the irrational and apparently chaotic moments of the historical process. Levelling itself could then be seen as a means of heightening the urgency of individuation. Indeed, one Danish commentator has even spoken of a 'utopistic' element in Kierkegaard's thought in the mid-1840s, suggesting that he was looking to the triumph of levelling in the external world as a necessary precursor to a reawakening of genuinely interior faith.[1] Thus, in the modern (levelling and post-levelling) age, faith must become once more a matter of individual decision and risk, ventured without the support of external guidelines and without the backing of a generally acknowledged community of faith. The modern believer must deliberately join the ranks of what he must know in advance to be a cognitive minority. There can be no ready-made map of the spiritual life to show what the next step must be, for the realm of faith, and the language of faith, is simply unintelligible to those whose world is formed by the concepts and categories of post-Enlightenment humanity.

The quality of unrecognizableness which in this way characterizes religious existence in the modern age is, however, more than just a result of the secularization of thought. Just as levelling paradoxically serves to emphasize the individual nature of the leap of faith, so the unrecognizableness of faith is an appropriate response to the God revealed in Christ, a God who came 'incognito'.

... And thus it is unrecognizableness, the absolute unrecognizableness, if one is God also to be an individual human being. To be the individual human being or an individual human being ... is the greatest possible, the infinite qualitative remove from being God, and therefore the most profound incognito ... The majority of people now living in Christendom live their lives in the illusion that if they had lived at the same time as Christ they would immediately have recognized him for who he was despite his unrecognizability ... it completely escapes them that this opinion (which they admittedly intend as an honour to Christ) is blasphemy ... he was truly God and therefore God *precisely to the degree* that he was unrecognizable as such, so that it was not flesh and blood but the opposite of flesh and blood that enabled Peter to recognize him. (PC, pp. 127–8)

For the Christian, entering into the unrecognizability of faith is more than bowing to the dominion of the secular outlook: it is itself a participating in the divine incognito. Freedom, individuality, personal responsibility, the religious life – all these have the form of unrecognizability because they exist as or are based on a response to the divine ground of personality revealed uniquely in the absolute incognito of an individual life.

The Structures of Selfhood

The believer's leap into the uncharted territory of faith is not seen by Kierkegaard as the abandonment of true humanity but as the moment of awakening to the true life of the self. Despite his radical emphasis on the indescribability of the leap he does go a long way towards identifying the structures of selfhood within which and in relation to which the leap occurs. His most concise technical definition of the self can be found in the psychological treatise *The Sickness Unto Death*:

> Man is spirit. But what is spirit? Spirit is the self. But what is the self? The self is a relationship which relates itself to itself, or it is that in the relationship by which the relationship relates itself to itself; the self is not the relationship but the fact that the relationship relates itself to itself. (SUD, p. 13)

This obviously needs careful unpacking – but its teaching is perhaps less esoteric than at first appears.

In common with the mainstream of idealist thought of his time Kierkegaard sees human existence as definable in terms of a sequence of dialectical or relational polarities, for example, infinity and finitude, absolute and relative, freedom and necessity, spirit and immediacy, eternity and time. It is characteristic of human existence, as opposed to the life of God or of nature, that it can only be understood when both sides of each of these polarities are brought into play. God can be characterized as infinite, absolute, free, spiritual, eternal being, and nature as finite, etc., but human existence is always both infinite and yet finite, in time and yet related to the eternal, free and yet subjected to necessity.

However, although we can never escape the tensions implicit in this situation, the relationship between the polarities of existence can take various forms. The essential factor is, as Kierkegaard puts it, that 'the self is not the relationship but that the relationship relates itself to itself'. In other words, the balance between the polarities of being is not something which just happens to us, not a part of our natural constitution, but is something for which we are, or are called to be, responsible. The relation must relate itself to its own self. We become selves only by an act of freedom. However, this freedom is a finite freedom since finitude, after all, belongs to its constitution and it cannot therefore be absolutely self-creating. It must acknowledge its dependence on God in the sense that 'in relating itself to itself and in willing to be itself, the self rests transparently in the power that established it' (SUD, p. 14).

The failure to do this is characterized by Kierkegaard as the state of despair, a condition he regards as virtually universal. 'And in any case there has lived no one and there lives no one outside Christendom who is not in despair, and in Christendom no one, as far as he is not a true Christian, and in so far as he is not quite that, he is none the less somewhat in despair' (SUD, p. 22). But even in the situation of despair, even in failing to bring about the freely willed synthesis that makes us what we truly are, we remain free and thus answerable for our predicament. To understand that that responsibility is a responsibility before God and yet still to fail to become who we are created and called to be is, in Kierkegaard's view, the essence of sin. Despair itself is thus fundamentally identical with sin.

The state of despair may take a variety of forms, and Kierkegaard, both in *The Sickness Unto Death* and in many other works, offers a number of careful and sometimes quite extensive analyses of them.

A person may, for instance, become lost by overemphasizing the infinite dimension of existence. This is the situation of the aesthetic, imaginative personality for whom imagination has come to act as a substitute for the concreteness of finite everyday reality. Conversely, it is possible to be in despair by lacking the sense for infinity, a lack which 'is desperate limitedness and narrow-mindedness' (SUD, p. 33). Kierkegaard comments on this form of despair that it

> is virtually never noticed in the world. Such a man, just by losing himself in this way, has attained the perfect condition for getting on in business affairs, indeed to being successful in the world. There is no hindrance here, no difficulty caused by concern for the self and its infinite destiny, he is polished as smooth as a pebble, as exchange-

able as a coin in circulation. Far from anyone seeing him as a man in despair he is regarded as being just what he should be. (SUD, p. 34)

Such a person is the typical bourgeois philistine of the present age – but religiously such a one is no worse off than the hyperimaginative personality who has failed to get to grips with life. In each case the authentically human synthesis is lacking. Both are equally in despair and both remain equally responsible for their situation.

This analysis of selfhood also suggests how the characterization of the present age is implicitly religious. For in the present age the range of qualities correlated with finitude are seen as being objectified by the systematic rationalizing of both theory and social practice and thus come to constitute the total frame of reference for human self-understanding. The present age is the totalitarianism of the finite mind and its deification of the established order asserts the finality of this attempt to define humanity by excluding everything that belongs to or recalls the passion for the infinite. But if only one half of what belongs to true humanity is repressed in this way it will inevitably lead to neurosis, to a situation in which the neglected aspect of reality reasserts its rights with a violence and one-sidedness proportionate to the degree of repression. The bourgeois age is thus at one and the same time an age in which the finite concerns of politics, business and family life shape the main contours of the social world – and also the age of the anarchic romantic rebel. The philistine household begets a brood of vagrant artists and nihilists. But this transformation is by no means creative, for it is powered by a fundamental lack, by the failure to be what we are planned to be. Far from revolutionizing society, it just leads us further and further from ourselves.

To transcend the categories of finitude must necessarily appear as a flight from reality, but in Kierkegaard's view it is a necessary step if we are to attain true wholeness of being, for it is only in its relation to infinity that finitude (that is, our worldly life) can be truly seen for what it is. In faith we come to ourselves and become 'transparent' to ourselves. Faith is an 'infinite reflection' which 'is nothing alien, but immediacy's transparency to itself' (SLW, p. 414). In such a state of transparency the finite world sees itself as it truly is, without distortion. Such vision is seen by Kierkegaard as an integral part of faith and a precondition of right action.

As the sea, when it thus lies still and deeply transparent, longs for heaven; so longs the pure heart, when it is still and deeply transparent, for the Good ... As the sea reflects the vault of heaven in its pure depths, so does the heart, when it has become still and deeply transparent, reflect the heavenly exaltation of the Good in its pure depths. (UDVS, p. 121)

In transparency we become open to ourselves and to God. It is a 'repetition' in which the content of the finite life is not abolished but grasped in its true spiritual significance. It is the key to living ethically.

Let us now once and for all compare an ethical and an aesthetic individual. The chief difference, on which everything turns, is this, that the ethical individual is transparent to himself and does not live *ins Blaue hinein*, as the aesthetic individual does. With this difference we have the whole picture. He who lives ethically has seen himself, knows himself, permeates the whole of his concrete situation with consciousness, allowing no indefinite thoughts to flutter around in him, no tempting possibilities to distract him with their conjuring tricks ... (EO 2, p. 258)

The way in which the polarities of existence become transparent to each other in faith can be illustrated by looking at Kierkegaard's treatment of the relationship between time and eternity. Human existence, he argues, is inescapably temporal, not just in an objective sense but in the sense that, subjectively, human life has meaning only in the context of the past from which it comes and the future towards which it goes. Above all, however, the active, willing character of human existence makes the future the pre-eminent temporal focus of meaning and significance; the meaning of our lives lies hidden in the goals and projects that we establish as our proximate future. Tell me your wish and I will tell you who you are! Those who lack such concern for the future are incapable of gaining the perspective of a fully mature human life.

Without knowing how they are in the midst of life's movement, one link in the chain that joins past and future; unconcerned as to how it happens they are carried along on the wave of the present ... for them life has no riddle, and yet their life is a riddle, a dream. (EUD, p. 33)

To be a link in the chain or a wave in the ocean does not, Kierkegaard maintains, constitute an authentically human life. Human existence is essentially future-directed. It is purposive. Personality and character in the full sense depend on the ability to expect something from life, and however many different expectations people may have, some hopeful, some fearful, all are in one way or another orientated towards the future, and it is this openness to the future that makes existence truly human.

The temporality with which Kierkegaard is concerned is obviously not clock-time, the measurable passing of time which affects the rest of creation as much as it affects human beings. It is the existential time, the time which carries and which is moulded by the projects through which we define ourselves. It is what later existentialists would call the 'historicity' of human existence. It is not, however, a matter of external history, but of what Kierkegaard calls 'internal history'. 'History first becomes true history when it becomes internal history,' he says, 'but true history fights with that which is the life principle of history with time' (EO 2, p. 134). In inwardness time expresses its essential significance as the form of inner intuition (Kant), the ever-present condition of subjective feeling and awareness. External history, on the other hand (and the aesthetic consciousness which corresponds to the external appearances of events), concentrates the consciousness of time in events which are also events in the visual field of space. A merely external view of history will inevitably tend towards spatialized conceptions of time. The meaning of the event of Napoleon is concentrated in the image of the conqueror on the white charger or in some other appearance which the life of Napoleon generated. But these external images of the events of a historical life do not reveal the essential historicity of man's being-in-time.

> If I wanted to portray a hero who conquers kingdoms and lands, then it could be excellently depicted in the moment, but a cross-bearer who takes up his cross day by day, can never be portrayed, neither by poetry nor by art, because the point is that he does it every day. Courage lets itself be very well concentrated in the moment but patience does not, because patience strives with time. (EO 2, p. 135)

To remain with the external appearance of events is, then, to fail to penetrate into the inner mystery of time. The task of internal history is to transcend the experience of time which culminates in the quasi-spatialized concept of the great moment or event. What is required is to become 'older than the moment' – and it is this which enables him to grasp the eternal (EUD, p. 86). Authentic temporality is not just a matter of making great resolutions or heroic acts of the will on the spur of the moment. Rather it is a matter of keeping these resolutions and sustaining them through time. Indeed, making an impressive decision in the heat of the moment can very well be yet another way of fantasizing away the real demands of our essential temporality.

> No, one goes on all fours before one learns to walk, and to want to fly is always suspicious. Certainly there are great decisions, but even in relation to these it is especially true that one should always be clear about one's resolve, so that one does not become such a high-flyer that one forgets how to walk. (EUD, p. 349)

The relation to time which characterizes faith is that of patience, a term which Kierkegaard used in the titles of three of his edifying discourses: 'To Acquire One's Soul in Patience', 'To Preserve One's Soul in Patience', and 'Patience in Expectation'. In the first of these he takes great pains to argue that patience is not simply a 'means' to the end of acquiring a true consciousness of selfhood, but to become patient is itself 'to acquire one's soul'. Patience is the sacrament of eternity in relation to time, the courage to bear the burden of the temporality which is intrinsic to human subjectivity. In patience, or in seeking to become patient, we do not struggle with an external obstacle but with time itself, yet at the same time the constancy of patience manifests the power of the eternal: 'If, then, there is something eternal in a human being, it must be able to exist and one must be able to require it in each and every changing scene of life' (UDVS, p. 11). This is what patience achieves. Patience is the constant renewal of the will which carries our resolve forward into the future. It is time qualified by eternity.

> How then should we go out to meet the future? When the sailor is out at sea, when everything changes all around him, when the waves rise and fall, he does not stare down into them, because they are constantly changing. He looks up to the stars. And why? Because they are faithful: they stood where they are now in our forefathers' time and shall stand there for those who come after us. How then does he conquer that which changes? By means of the eternal. By means of the eternal one conquers the future, because the eternal is the basis of the future. (EUD, p. 19)

The eternal does not destroy the temporality of human life but brings it to its fullest expression. It does not abolish our expectation, our concern for the future, but it transforms this future into 'the incognito in which the eternal, as incommensurable for time, none the less wills to be involved with time' (CA, p. 89). The moment is not left as an almost spatialized atom of time but becomes 'that ambiguous relationship in which time and eternity touch one another ...' (CA, p. 89). The relation of faith to time is thus one of patient resolve, a relation which articulates the union of the temporal and eternal poles of human existence. In this way time becomes, in Plato's phrase, a 'moving image of eternity'. To be concerned with eternity is not therefore to seek to escape from time. On the contrary, the more we accept our essential temporality and face up to the sheer impermanence of all human (and of all finite, creaturely) life, the closer we draw to eternity. We do not come into relationship with the absolute by absolutizing the finite world but by recognizing our real nothingness and transiency 'before God'.

This analysis of temporality is paralleled by Kierkegaard's treatment of the other polarities of being. In each case it is the free affirmation of the relatedness of the polarities which actualizes our essential selfhood. None the less, in the context of a one-dimensional society in which humanity is understood only in terms of the categories of finitude this journey to selfhood must appear to be a leap into the dark, a journeying into nothingness, into a realm which has no meaning and, in effect, no existence in the closed world of the practical man with his business, his science and his politics. In the situation of modernity the polarities of our true being are separated by a veritable abyss – a fact which is as true for the hyperspiritual aesthete as it is for the down-to-earth bourgeois family man – and to seek the union in which true being consists one must venture out into this abyss or void. But from the standpoint of faith this void is the matrix of a paradoxical reversal of consciousness. It is in accepting our failure to be what we are called to be that we find in ourselves the new immediacy, the new creation, the purity of heart which wills one thing and in its profound transparency reflects the gathering of our fragmented being into a new unity. Faith is not the mere mirror-image of materialism, but overcomes the conflict between materialism and spiritualism, although it does so in a way and at a level that is altogether non-objective. In other words, a complete break with the thought patterns of the modern objectifying world-view is required, not so as to enter into an object-less subjectivity (which Kierkegaard accused the Romantics of doing), but as a corrective measure by which to heal the imbalance in the self brought about by the colossal preponderance of objectivity in the present age.

Angst: Some Case-Histories

Although Kierkegaard offers us no 'map' of the leap of faith by which we become subjective, he does offer a number of case-histories which illuminate and exemplify what this can involve. The form of these case-histories is typically psychological rather than theological or philosophical, and the Kierkegaardian category of 'angst' invariably plays a key role. 'Angst' is not to be confused with despair, although there are important connections between the two conditions. 'Angst' is, essentially, the psychological state of a person whose freedom is present to them only as a possibility. It is the call for freedom that the subject has not yet acknowledged or acted upon – or, in some cases, refuses to act upon. But even if we can avoid this call at the conscious level we cannot avoid it altogether since it comes to us from the deepest source of all reality, from God. 'Angst', then, is a manifestation of something lacking, an absence, an emptiness, which can none the less have devastating consequences for our psychological development. As an extreme example of such 'angst' Kierkegaard, via the pen of Assessor William, describes the emperor Nero. Nero has experienced all there is to experience in the way of worldly pleasure, but all this experience does not make him psychologically mature. Instead he is fixed in an infantile condition in which he is haunted by intimations of a higher life that he constantly represses.

> Then the spirit within him gathers itself like a dark cloud, its wrath broods over his soul, and it becomes 'angst' which does not cease even in the moment of pleasure. Look, that is why his gaze is so dark that no one can bear to behold it, his glance so blazing that it causes anxiety to the beholder, for behind the eye lies the soul like a shadow. One calls this glance an imperial glance, and the whole world shakes before it, and yet his inner being is angst. A child who looks at him in an unaccustomed way, a casual look, can frighten him, it is as if that person owned him: for the spirit wants to appear in him, wants him to possess himself in self-consciousness, but he cannot do it, and it is repressed and gathers new wrath. (EO 2, p. 186)

Nero is someone who cannot, will not grow up, and therefore cannot achieve the synthesis in which true selfhood subsists. Angst is the repressed awareness of the possibility we all essentially have to exist as freedom. 'The person who is educated by angst is educated by possibility, and only the person who is educated by possibility is educated as befits his infinity' (CA, p. 156). Such an education is a vertiginous experience, as what we are is touched by the whisper of what we might become.

> Angst can be compared to dizziness. He whose eye looks down into the abysmal depths grows dizzy. But the cause is as much in his looking as in the abyss itself, for it would not have happened if he had not looked down. Similarly angst is the dizziness caused by freedom which occurs when the spirit wills to bring about the synthesis, and freedom looks down into its own possibility ... (CA, p. 61)

In the state of angst we anticipate the freedom we are called to be as a possibility, as something which, as yet, does not exist, as a lack, an absence, a void, an abyss, a nothing. 'If we now ask more closely what the object of angst is, then the answer must as usual be that it is nothing. Angst and nothing stand in a constant reciprocal relation to one another' (CA, p. 96). 'But what effect does nothing have? It begets angst' (CA, p. 41).

It is important to note that whereas a philosopher such as Heidegger insists on separating the phenomenon of 'angst' from the realm of the concrete, everyday experiences of the existing subject, Kierkegaard compels us to see it as something which can be shatteringly real in the life of the individual.

Indeed, many of Kierkegaard's pseudonymous books as well as his religious discourses offer examples of how 'angst' can become real in actual life-situations. In *Repetition*, for example, he portrays a young man who loses all sense of meaning and purpose in life as the result of an unhappy love-affair for the break-up of which he holds himself responsible.

> My life has been brought to its breaking-point; I am tired of existence, it is tasteless, without salt or sense. Even if I were hungrier than Pierrot I wouldn't care to eat the explanation people offer. One sticks one's finger into the soil to be able to smell what land one is in: I stick my finger into existence – it smells of nothing. Where am I? What does it mean to say: the world? What does this word signify? Who has tricked me into all this and now leaves me here? (FT/R, p. 200)

The fullest of these case-histories, however, is the case of the nameless diarist of *Stages on Life's Way*. We have already seen how Kierkegaard uses this so-called 'Quidam' to illustrate the ultimately self-destructive nature of a life which tries to base itself on aesthetic principles. But as Quidam's encounter with the self's possibility of freedom brings about a dizzying fall into the abyss of infinite possibility and he collapses in on his own nothingness, he is also faced with the religious challenge to accept himself and receive forgiveness from the hand of God. We never learn whether Quidam does finally achieve the wholeness and the freedom which he so despairingly seeks. The important thing, we are told, is not what happened to him – but whether we ourselves are going to find our own freedom and make for ourselves the leap of faith. Although he is scrupulous to an almost neurotic degree, Quidam's task is the task of each one of us, the task of the self to become what we are, to take responsibility for ourselves, for our past, for our guilt (even if we cannot always ourselves fathom out the extent to which we have acted rightly or wrongly), confident in the power of the forgiveness of sins and so to become transparent to ourselves in the new immediacy of faith. If this happens, then the encounter with the void becomes the beginning of the new creation.

The phenomenon of angst plays a key role in Kierkegaard's reinterpretation of the Genesis account of the fall. As he tells the story, angst is precisely the condition of Adam and Eve prior to the fall: a sense of freedom and of moral responsibility for good and evil that is none the less not yet actual. However, in the face of their dizzying possibility of freedom they 'grasp at finitude' (CA, p. 61), substituting a multitude of relative and material goals for the single-mindedness of spiritual freedom. This fall is subsequently re-enacted by each of us, as we slip from a state of angst, in which the prospect of freedom lies open before us, into one of despair, when freedom remains merely as the guilt and even sin accruing to our failure to be ourselves.

But angst is not merely a negative phenomenon. It is not identical with despair. On the contrary, while revealing the void that undermines all finite certainties it can serve to educate us up to faith. It is the vertigo of freedom but also the summons to assault the infinite. For faith, the nothingness of 'angst' is the narrow gate by which faith itself comes into being.

Kierkegaard comes back to the religious significance of the experience of our own nothingness in a number of his edifying discourses.

... if a man none the less understood how to make himself in truth what in truth he is: nothing; knew how to apply the seal of patience to what he understood – Oh! then his life, were it the greatest or the meanest, should this very day be joyful amazement and blessed wonder, and be so always, for there is only one who in truth is the eternal object of wonder, and he is God, only one who can prevent wonder, and he is man, when he will make himself something. (EUD, p. 226)

To become as nothing is thus seen by Kierkegaard as an essential step on the way to religious rebirth. In the discourse on 'Man's Need of God Constitutes his Highest Perfection', he sees this annihilation of the self as arising out of the struggle to achieve selfhood, to master one's own self. For the one who 'does not strive with the world, but with himself' (EUD, p. 308), the discovery is soon made that, as no one is stronger than themselves, one cannot, in fact, overcome or transform oneself, cannot, of one's own power, bring about the actualization of the freedom which is sought. 'Thus he can achieve absolutely nothing ... this is a man's annihilation, and this annihilation is his truth' (EUD, p. 309). It is only in the light of this realization that we become capable of learning that it is God and God alone who can do all things: unless or until we reach this point, there will always be the suspicion that it is we ourselves who are the covert manipulators of the God-relationship.

Perhaps the most lyrical expression of this idea is in the discourse 'He who Prays rightly Strives in Prayer with God and Wins – by this: that God Wins.'

Yet whom should the one who strives wish to be like other than God; but if he himself is something or wants to be something, then this something is enough to prevent the likeness from appearing. Only when he himself becomes nothing, only then can God shine through him, so that he comes to be like God. However great he is otherwise, he cannot express God's likeness, God can only impress himself on him when he himself has become nothing. It is precisely when the sea exercises all its might that it cannot reflect the image of the heavens above, and even the smallest movement means that it does not reflect it quite purely; but when it becomes still and deep then heaven's image sinks down into its nothingness. (EUD, p. 399)

In this way the human being is 'transfigured in God'. To become nothing is to enter into communion with the one who is all in all, and to have restored in us the image and likeness of God obliterated in the fall. This is not, however, to be understood as a fusion or confusion of divine and human being. The truly spiritual relationship to God is one of adoration and praise.

> But God is spirit, invisible, and the image of the invisible is also invisible: thus the invisible creator mirrors himself in the invisibility which is the quality of spiritual existence, and God's image is precisely the invisible glory ... To be spirit is man's invisible glory ... To walk upright was a distinction, but to be able to cast oneself down in worship is yet more glorious, and the whole of nature is like a great company of servants who are here to remind man, their master, to worship God ... It is glorious to be clad like the lilies; it is still more glorious to be the lord of creation who walks upright; but it is most glorious of all to be as nothing in worship. (UDVS, pp. 192–3)

Through becoming as nothing, humanity is restored to a right relation both to creation and to the creator, becoming what we truly are or are called to be. This means that the traditional antinomies between faith and works, nature and grace, are set aside, or at least put in their right perspective: our supreme 'work' is to become nothing, to surrender all striving, the wilful battle to escape the bondage of the will – and precisely by means of and in this surrender to find faith in the providential and redemptive power of God; similarly, the saving grace which meets us in the experience of our own nothingness is seen by Kierkegaard as the grace of the creator who in restoring us to ourselves restores us to our rightful place in creation. In asceticism the individual only finds the self in isolation from others, in mysticism he only finds an abstract self, isolated from the cares and concerns of worldly existence, but in faith 'the individual then chooses himself as a concretion determined in many ways' (EO 2, pp. 250–1). That is to say that in the synthesis of freedom we rediscover our finitude, our temporality, our place in the world as particular individuals with particular obligations, tasks and relationships – and so the paradox of grace is that it makes us truly ourselves as if for the first time and establishes us in a context of finite creatureliness. This is seen by Kierkegaard as a direct consequence of the fact that in achieving the full realization of freedom, in 'choosing' one's self, one does not create one's self, but 'chooses it absolutely from the hand of the eternal God' (EO 2, p. 217).

Selfhood and Faith

However, this account of the journey towards selfhood leaves many questions unanswered. For instance, is Kierkegaard saying that the act of self-choice, in nothingness before God, is something we can ourselves achieve? Although I have suggested that Kierkegaard himself offers 'becoming as nothing' as a way of short-circuiting traditional argu- ments about faith and works, a suspicion may yet remain that it is none the less a kind of 'work'. Moreover, what is the relationship between becoming who we are in the inwardness of the self and the saving relation to God by faith in Christ? In other words: what is the relationship between the paradoxical unity of the polarities of being within the human subject and the paradox historically given to faith in the God-man Jesus Christ?

These questions are importantly connected. If we could become who we are by the exertion of our wills, then it is hard to see what need there would be for any saving action on the part of God. Thus, although Assessor William is clearly no absolute idealist (and still less a materialist of the Feuerbachian kind), he seems relatively optimistic as to our capacity to choose our way out of the situation of despair, and it is therefore no surprise that although he does speak of God the creator, he says little of Christ, or God the redeemer. We cannot create ourselves on his view of things, but we do seem to have the ability to put ourselves back into the right relation to God that characters such as the aesthete 'A' have squandered.

The recommendation found throughout the edifying discourses to become as nothing is harder to read. On the one hand it is clear that when we become as nothing the will, no less than the intellect, must be suspended. The saving action comes to us as grace. We cannot manipulate God into transfiguring our nothingness, precisely because it is a condition in which we accept that we can do nothing of ourselves. On the other hand, the process that brings us to such nothingness is one that we do indeed set in motion, as we seek to rescue our personality from immersion in the stream of worldly life. Perhaps, then, we can bring ourselves into a condition of nothingness: but whether we are able to experience that condition as renewal or as grace is not within our power.

The advent of Christ, however, must come to us from outside. As the paradox, it transcends both reason and will. Yet it is not completely unrelated to our human situation. As the appearing of the God in time, in, with and under all the circumstances of creaturely existence it establishes the hope of a real fulfilment of our human potential. It is striking that whereas *Philosophical Fragments* constructs an account of the incarnation purely hypothetically, in order to bring into focus the ideological differences between idealism and Christianity, the *Concluding Unscientific Postscript* tries to show how faith in the incarnation answers to human needs. In the *Postscript*'s own terminology, it supplements the purely 'dialectical' approach of the *Fragments* with a 'pathos-filled' approach, showing how the requirement to exist as spirit impacts upon human existence.

That we exist not merely 'before God' but before the God who comes to us in, with and under the conditions of existence, is, in a term used in *The Sickness Unto Death*, the criterion that shows the measure both of our despair and of the hope that is set before us. It signals the highest possible valuation of human life: that we are those for whom the God consented to take flesh, suffer and die. In the words of a fifteenth-century carol: 'Now [now, that is, in the light of the incarnation] man is made of full great price.' Kierkegaard makes the point by means of a parable:

> Were I to imagine a poor casual labourer and the mightiest emperor who ever lived, and that this most mighty emperor suddenly took it into his mind to send for the labourer, who had never even dreamed and 'in whose heart it had never arisen' that the emperor knew that he existed, then he would account himself indescribably fortunate just once to be allowed to see the emperor, something he would certainly tell to his children and grandchildren about as the most important event of his life – but now imagine that the emperor sent for him and gave it to be known that he wanted him as a son-in-law, what then? Then the labourer would quite naturally be pretty well confused, embarrassed and troubled by it. It would ... seem to him to be something queer, crazy even, something that he would in no way dare to discuss with anybody, since he himself was near to thinking that the real reason for this was what his friends and neighbours would straightway make much ado about: that the emperor wanted to make a fool of him, so that he, the labourer, would become the laughing-stock of the whole town ... Now let us assume that it was no outer reality [such as becoming the emperor's son-in-law] that was being considered, but something inward, so that there were no facts that could help the labourer be sure [as to what really was the case], but faith itself was the only fact at issue so that the whole matter was dependent on faith, on whether he was

sufficiently courageous to have the humility to believe it ... How
many labourers might there be who would have such courage?
(SUD, pp. 84–5)

The incarnation, taken in its full doctrinal sense, gives to human life an
incomparable dignity and value. But are that dignity and that value
justified? Are they 'real'? Kierkegaard's last word seems to be that such a
question simply cannot be decided objectively, apart from the passion of
faith. Whether our hearts will indeed find their rest in God (Augustine),
whether life is no more than a useless passion (Sartre), whether the
perfection of humanity in Christ is divine revelation or merely a 'focus
imaginarius' (Kant) – all these are possible outcomes, and the believer
can never be insured against the risk that he is behaving like a casual
labourer who imagines himself to be the emperor's chosen son-in-law.

Where does this leave the question of faith and works?

Perhaps the best answer is that it leaves it in suspension since, on
Kierkegaard's terms, it is a question that just doesn't make sense. For, if
faith is all we have to go on, then we can never know whether our faith is
simply a matter of human resolve to see life 'as if' destined for adoption
as a child of God or whether it is a real response to the call of God. If the
Christian gospel is true, then faith is indeed 'faith' in the sense of a
response to grace. If it is not true, then faith is nothing but a human
'work'. But since faith is precisely the way in which (and the only way in
which) we can hold the gospel to be true, we can never get behind it to
see who or what is really pulling the levers. We can only believe – or, as
Kierkegaard constantly reminds us, be offended. But if we do believe,
then we will – and must – be convinced that all is of grace.

Individuality and Community

Another important issue connected with Kierkegaard's view of faith is
that of the extent of his individualism. In other words: does Kierkegaardian faith lead us away from the reality of the world of everyday
social experience? Not if it is accepted that Kierkegaard's insistence on
the concreteness of self-choice means that to come to one's self is to
become a self which exists socially and which is genuinely capable of
free relationships with others and, indeed, that it is only such individ-
uated selves who are truly capable of real community and who are the
real, if usually unacknowledged, 'pillars of society', the hidden 'just
men' whose righteousness (and, especially, whose righteous suffering)
counterbalances the injustices of the human social order. We may recall

what was said in the previous chapter regarding Kierkegaard's critique of contemporary social life where he asserted that 'the cohesiveness of community comes from each one's being a single individual ... Every single individual in community guarantees the community ... In a public there is no single individual, and the whole is nothing' (JP 2952). The 'individual' points to other possibilities of social being than those which are evidenced in the anomie of mass-society. We can illustrate this by referring again to Kierkegaard's portrayal of 'the Seducer', for the protest against the aesthetic way of life as exemplified in 'the Seducer' is not merely a moral protest against a 'bad' man who flouts traditional standards of behaviour. The Seducer is rather seen as a pitiable character who for all his many encounters never really encounters another individual, never enters into a relationship of mutual responsibility and mutual openness. His relationships are exclusively 'I – It' rather than 'I – Thou'. He is, in the last resort, a prisoner of his own narcissism, incapable of breaking through to a vision of the essential other, confined to the voyeuristic vision of spiritual adolescence. Like Quidam, the Seducer is, as an extreme case, atypical – and yet he is very much a representative of the decisive character-traits of the modern age of reflection as Kierkegaard understands it.

Of all Kierkegaard's writings, *Works of Love* is most frequently used to support the claim that Kierkegaard's thought is fundamentally 'social'. Here Kierkegaard insists repeatedly on the need for faith to bear fruit in our comportment towards others. So – in a slightly confused simile – Kierkegaard explains how the 'hidden inwardness' of faith will inevitably affect the social existence of the individual.

> As the depths of the quiet lake are grounded in the hidden spring which no eye can see, so human love is grounded still more deeply in God's love ... As the quiet lake entices you to look at it, but by its dark reflection prevents you from seeing down through it: just so does love's mysterious origin in God's love prevent you from seeing its ground ... Thus is love's life hidden; but this hidden life is itself in motion, and has eternity within it. Like the quiet lake, which, however still it is on the surface, is none the less really running water, because its source is the hidden spring: so love, however quiet it is in its hiddenness, is nevertheless flowing ... this hidden life of love is recognizable by its *fruits*. (WL, p. 10)

Kierkegaard also makes the connection between the individual discovery of selfhood and the life of love by reflecting on Christ's injunction to love our neighbours 'as ourselves'. This, Kierkegaard points out, 'presupposes that every man loves himself' (WL, p. 17),

> If anyone, therefore refuses to learn from Christianity to love himself in the right way, still less can he love his neighbour ... To love one's self in the right way and to love one's neighbour stand in a completely reciprocal relationship to one another, and are basically one and the same thing. (WL, p. 22)

In discovering our essential freedom in and through the realization of our nothingness before God we discover the 'divine equality' among humankind. It is only through such an absolute and inward 'levelling' that we realize the radical nature of the demand to see each and every one of our fellow human beings as a 'neighbour' in the Christian sense. Through this experience the external distinctions of rank, riches and renown are seen, in Kierkegaard's phrase, as nothing more than a 'disguise' concealing the essential common humanity. Kierkegaard regards the modern preoccupation with levelling in the external sense (the removal of external distinctions by political and economic strategies) as fundamentally denying this underlying common humanity. Such attempts at social engineering are trapped in ways of thinking that see the external differences as having a decisive significance for human life. Only radical inwardness, on the other hand, liberates us to see each and every other person as 'neighbour'. 'To love one's neighbour, as he is, with all the earthly difference just as it is, is ... essentially to wish to be equally available for every man unconditionally' (WL, pp. 83–4). Only in this way can the envious and fearful spirit of comparison, a spirit which constantly accentuates the external differences and distinctions between men, be overcome.

Nevertheless, it is hard to maintain an appropriate tension between God-centred and human-centred love, and the claim that *Works of Love* offers a 'social' view of faith is not uncontested. Indeed, some would see it as systematically stripping the word 'love' of any empirical, social sense it might have, such is its emphasis on getting the God-relationship right prior to any particular human 'works of love'.

Here Martin Buber's critique of Kierkegaard is relevant. Buber acknowledges, although with some reservations, that Kierkegaard's vision of 'the individual' does not exclude fundamental relationships with others but can act as the foundation for such relationships. 'Not before a man can say I in perfect reality – that is, finding himself – can he in perfect reality say *Thou* – that is, to God.'[2] In this, Buber believes,

Kierkegaard is on firm biblical ground. The self-knowledge which Kierkegaard commends is not meant in the Greek, Socratic sense (despite Kierkegaard's own copious use of Socrates as a model for his life's work); rather, 'the goal of this becoming is not the "right" life, but the entry into a relation'.[3]

None the less, Buber discerns a tension here. On the one hand this relation very often seems to involve a concern with God to the exclusion of concern for the world, something Buber cannot accept. On the other hand, 'No one can so refute Kierkegaard as Kierkegaard himself', and, he suggests, Kierkegaard himself tells us that

> The Single One, if he really believes, and that means if he really is a Single One ... can and may have to do essentially with another. And behind this there lurks the extreme that he who can also *ought* to do this. 'The only means by which God communicates with man is the ethical.' But the ethical in its plain truth means to help God by loving his creation in his creatures, by loving it towards him.[4]

The category of the individual, whatever Kierkegaard himself ultimately did with it, and whatever Kierkegaard's private individual tragedy may suggest (matters we shall look at in the following chapter), is not, Buber is saying, in any way incompatible with a profound concern for community and responsibility towards others.

> The Single One who lives in his relation of faith must wish to have it fulfilled in the uncurtailed measure of the life he lives. He must face the hour which approaches him, the biographical and historical hour, just as it is, in its whole world content and apparently senseless contradiction, without weakening the impact of otherness in it.[5]

A possible convergence between Kierkegaard, the prophet of the individual, and Buber, the prophet of relationship (who was none the less a passionate reader of Kierkegaard), can be illustrated less abstrusely. In a personal (if somewhat fictionalized) anecdote Buber recounts how he came to give up a purely ecstatic, other-worldly kind of religiosity:

> ... one forenoon, after a morning of 'religious' enthusiasm, I had a visit from an unknown young man, without being there in spirit. I certainly did not fail to let the meeting be friendly ... I conversed attentively and openly with him – only I omitted to guess the

questions which he did not put. Later, not long after, I learned from
one of his friends – he himself was no longer alive – the essential
content of these questions; I learned that he had come to me not
casually, but borne by destiny, not for a chat but for a decision. He
had come to me, he had come in this hour. What do we expect when
we are in despair and yet go to a man? Surely a presence by which we
are told that nevertheless there is a meaning. Since then I have given
up the 'religious' which is nothing but the exception, extraction,
exaltation, ecstasy ... I possess nothing but the everyday out of
which I am never taken.[6]

In *Purity of Heart* Kierkegaard speaks of a man who is struggling to
find faith in divine providence as a compensation for the conflict and
suffering he has experienced in his own life. He eagerly expects help
from God, but what happens?

> ... perhaps the help is delayed; instead there comes a sufferer to him
> whom he can help. But this sufferer finds him impatient, distant; this
> sufferer must be satisfied with the excuse: 'that he is not at this
> moment in the position or in the mood to concern himself with
> others' sufferings, as he himself is facing adversity.' And yet he
> thinks that he has faith, faith that there is a loving providence which
> uses human beings as its instruments. (UDVS, p. 69)

The discovery of the individual which lies at the end of the journey
through nothingness is an illusion if it does not include the discovery of
human solidarity: solidarity in community, in suffering and in our need
of God. Kierkegaard offers neither a moral nor a political programme
for reforming the age of reflection. What he offers is a way to reach the
inward foundations which any reform must presuppose if it is genuinely
going to preserve the life-giving springs of human primitivity. The
materialistic self-assertiveness of the age should not lead us to forget
that all human life is tied to the existence of finite, transient and pre-
eminently fallible individuals, and that real love and real sociality must
bear within itself a recognition of this fragility.

SEVEN

DOCTOR OR PATIENT?

THE TREMENDOUS EMPHASIS on subjectivity and on the actuality of the individual life as the context and ultimate criterion of truth in Kierkegaard's thought made it almost inevitable that his own personal life would be drawn into his writing to an extent that rarely happens in theology or philosophy. Moreover, when Kierkegaard's influence began to spread outside Denmark at the end of the nineteenth century it did so in association with the movement in literary criticism spearheaded by George Brandes which regarded the author's biographical and social situation as determinative for any assessment of his work. It was in fact Brandes himself who wrote the first serious monograph on Kierkegaard's work (just as he was also the first to bring Nietzsche's writing to the attention of a European public). As a result a great deal of Kierkegaard interpretation has shown an almost obsessive concern with his personal life, either using his works (published and unpublished alike) to reconstruct his psychological development or using what was known (or assumed to be known) about his life to explain problematic aspects of his writing. This has on occasion led to quite fanciful results. While it is clear, for instance, that Kierkegaard's own experience of an unhappy love affair provided him with much of the material which he worked into Quidam's diary in *Stages on Life's Way*, it is equally clear that he fictionalized this experience in such a way that it is impossible for us to read the text as straight autobiography. In his first published work, *From the Papers of One Still Living*, he had castigated Hans Christian Andersen's novels on the grounds that they reflected the author's life too intimately, so that they read more like amputated segments of the author's life than like literary productions (EPW, p. 84). Indeed, few writers have been more aware of the interaction between reality and illusion, revelation and concealment in all literary work than Kierkegaard. Even the figure of himself which Kierkegaard reveals through the multitude of pseudonyms is strongly fictionalized, being only one aspect, one possibility of Kierkegaard the man and in no way the man himself in his actual concrete individuality. This is even true if we turn to his voluminous journals and papers. In the past these have been read as sources for filling in what would otherwise be the gaps in our knowledge of his biography. But here too it turns out that the relationship between revelation and concealment, between fact and fiction is almost unfathomably complex. The Danish critic Henning Fenger has convincingly demonstrated that many passages from the journals (especially the early journals) which were once regarded as straight diaristic accounts of Kierkegaard's own life and thought cannot be so and should rather be read as sketches and notes for never-completed literary works. Fenger subtitles his book 'De Omnibus Dubitandum': everything is to be doubted.[1]

None the less, it is almost impossible to banish Kierkegaard himself from his works entirely. They bear the impress of a highly personal, highly impassioned mind, a mind which seeks to persuade us that neither literature nor philosophy can ever ultimately be cut off from the depths of life by which they are formed and nourished. These pages could only have been written by this man who lived at this time in this country, who experienced these particular events and who performed these particular actions. In commending the acceptance of our unique and unavoidably particular contingency as the matrix of the religious life Kierkegaard's works themselves bear all the marks of such particularity and contingency, and we cannot understand them altogether without in some measure penetrating into the unique specificity of the life which gave birth to them.

But when we do turn to Kierkegaard's life the problems with which the works confront us are compounded by the oddity of that life, the peculiarity of its cares and obsessions and the depths of isolation and unhappiness which it reveals. In *The Sickness Unto Death* Kierkegaard speaks of all Christian writing as being analogous to the words of a doctor attending a sick patient, but can this self-confessed melancholic be taken seriously in the role of doctor to the age? Is he not rather more suited to the role of patient, one who is himself in need of the liberation that modern materialistic psychology makes available?

Such questions are raised by the works themselves. For while the way of individuation according to Kierkegaard involves what he calls the double-movement of renunciation and affirmation, the annihilation of the self that is also the paradoxical moment in which we come to ourselves for the first time, it is more and more the case in the development of his authorship that the 'movements of infinity', the moments of renunciation or annihilation, are emphasized to the detriment of the counter-movement, the paradoxical affirmation of finitude which was exemplified in the fictional 'knight of faith'.

The sombre shadow of a world-denying form of religiosity makes its appearance early in the authorship but constantly grows in intensity and depth as the authorship continues. In *Either-Or* when the Assessor has finished drawing the contrast between the aesthetic attitude and his own ethical form of religiousness, he indicates the possibility of a third way by sending on to his young friend a copy of a sermon preached by a friend of his who is a pastor on the lonely Jutland Heath. The sermon is entitled 'The Edification Contained in the Thought that over against God we are always in the Wrong', and although the Assessor commends it as being a summary of the teaching he has himself tried to express there is an underlying tone of a darker, more mysterious, more sombre type of religion than the Assessor's optimistic life-view is able to express. *Fear and Trembling* explicitly addresses itself to the question as to whether there might not be a religious demand which not only transcends but even contradicts the ethical point of view, what Kierkegaard calls a 'teleological suspension of the ethical', that is, a suspension of ethical norms for the sake of a higher purpose. He chooses the story of Abraham and Isaac to illustrate what this might mean. For here is an example of someone being called by God to commit an action which not only breaks all human laws but also goes against what is elsewhere said to be divine law. More recent biblical criticism has, of course, suggested that the text can in fact be read precisely as an underscoring of the opposition of Israelite religion to the practice of child sacrifice which is widely evidenced in ancient Canaan. For Kierkegaard, however, it is essential that Abraham has to take seriously the divine command to take his only son and kill him. This is not, as Kierkegaard stresses, comparable to the case of a man who sacrifices life or goods for some social cause or some rationally defensible purpose, such as that of a resistance fighter who not only risks his own life but also incurs risks for all those associated with him: Abraham's action is and can only be motivated by an unfathomable sense of divine calling. Although Kierkegaard recognizes that, because Abraham did not actually have to kill Isaac, what we have in the story as a whole is a pattern of renunciation-and-affirmation, a giving-up that leads to a renewed giving from God, it is clear that his fascination with the story does not lie in the moment when Abraham receives Isaac again, but in the moment when he believingly responds to the demand to make the sacrifice. Abraham's predicament is something which no pragmatist, no man of common sense, no poet, no philosopher could ever understand or adequately portray. It lies altogether beyond the boundaries of human rationalization.

Similarly, in *Stages on Life's Way*, where the Assessor makes a second appearance, he concludes a lengthy discussion of marriage with some reflections on the possibility of whether, under certain conditions, there might not exist a valid form of religiosity which involves renouncing the world of family life and civic duty for a solitary, misunderstood and, humanly speaking, wretched existence. The man who is called to such a life will be, he conjectures, 'the most miserable man of all, a cast-off from humanity' (SLW, p. 181), but whether 'a kind of blessedness can take shape, whether a divine meaning can lie in this terrible nothingness' (SLW, p. 181) the Assessor does not know.

In Kierkegaard's later writings, in contrast to the emphasis on faith in the incarnate Christ in *Philosophical Fragments* and *Concluding Unscientific Postscript*, the relation to Christ is increasingly seen in terms of being willing to share with him the experience of rejection and of going with him on the way of the cross. Nor is this conceived of simply in terms of cross-centred devotional exercises. This following of the crucified is not just a mental or emotional following but is concrete discipleship in the actual conditions of the contemporary world. Although much of what Kierkegaard says on this subject is incredibly repetitive, he could on occasion indicate what this call to radical discipleship might mean in prose poems equal in standard to the best of the early pseudonymous works.

There was once a man. As a boy he was brought up strictly in the Christian religion. He did not hear much of that which children usually hear, about the little baby Jesus, the angels and suchlike. Rather they portrayed the Crucified one all the more often to him, so that this image was the only one he had and the only impression he had of the Saviour; although a child he was already as old as an old man. This image followed him through life, he never grew younger, and he never escaped from this image. As it is told of a painter whose anguished conscience could not stop looking back at the image of the murdered man which pursued him: just so was he, through love, unable to look away from this image even for a moment, as it drew him to itself ... Gradually, as he grew older, this image gained even more power over him. It seemed to him as if it were constantly demanding something from him. For he had always found it ungodly that anyone could try to paint this image, and equally ungodly to look at such a painted image aesthetically, to see if it was a good likeness – instead of oneself becoming the image of one who was like Him, and he was driven by an inexplicable force to want to be like Him, in so far as a man can be like Him. (PA, pp. 81–2)

This passage comes from a small treatise entitled 'Has a Man the Right to let Himself be put to Death for the Truth?', and although Kierkegaard answers the question with a clear 'no' (on the grounds that no one has the right to cause another person to become guilty of murder – except Christ, who, as the God-man, had the right on earth to forgive sins and thereby release those who murdered him from their guilt), the caution shown in this essay seems to have been ignored in his later writings. 'Christ is the Pattern and "imitation" follows from this. There is really only one true way of being a Christian, namely: to be a disciple. "The disciple" is characterized *inter alia* by this: that he suffers for the doctrine' (FSE/JY, p. 207). '"Imitation", "the imitation of Christ" is really the point where the human race winces, this is where the difficulty really hits home, here is where it really gets decided whether one will accept Christianity or not' (FSE/JY, p. 188). To be a Christian, then, is to imitate Christ, to go his way of rejection, humiliation and crucifixion – a point we have already seen Kierkegaard making in his attack on 'Christendom', especially in relation to Christendom's failure to live up to the ideal of the witness to the truth. If the humanistic theology of the last two centuries has tended to balk at this notion, there is a great deal in the New Testament and in the Christian tradition to support Kierkegaard on this. To be a Christian, then, is to be crucified with Christ, to die to the world. 'Christianity', Kierkegaard concludes, 'clearly considers suffering to be the mark of the God-relationship' (JP 4681). He even goes so far as to reduce Christianity to two theses: 'Because you are a sufferer, therefore God loves you ... Because you love God, therefore you must suffer' (JP 4688). The way of suffering and of being misunderstood is no longer, as in *Stages on Life's Way*, an exception to the rule but has itself become the only way, the norm, of religious life – '... without dying to the world you can never love God. It will be sheer agony for you ...' (JP 4690).

None the less, Kierkegaard clearly regarded both the excesses of asceticism and the cult of physical suffering as aberrations. The real Christ-like suffering was the suffering of love, of betrayal, of rejection by one's fellow men. In the discourse 'The Night in Which He was Betrayed' he reflected that 'Ah, but to betray – that is the most painful blow you can give to love; there is no pain, not even the most agonizing bodily pain, at which love winces in such depths of soul as at betrayal ...' (CD, p. 287). The real suffering of the Christian is the wedge that faith drives between himself and others: '... the collision man shrinks from the most, the collision with the others, having to suffer because by loving God one becomes unlike the others ... this collision, which actually is the animal-creature's greatest suffering, is the very one Christianity heads toward' (JP 4730). This is the ultimate reversal of the values of the modern 'mass-man'.

Writing of his own experience of public rejection and humiliation at the hands of *The Corsair*, a widely circulated satirical newspaper, he recognized that his own martyrdom was not like that of the early Christians who had to suffer the terrors of the arena: 'a martyrdom of laughter is what I really have suffered' (JP 6348).

> Without falsifying or muddling the concept, I may say that my life is a kind of martyrdom, but of a new type. What I, as a public person, am suffering, is best described as a slow death, like being trampled to death by geese, or like pettiness's painful method of execution used in distant lands: being cast to the insects, and the offender is first smeared with honey to whet the insects' appetite – and in the same way my reputation is the honey ... (JP 6906)

But the real pain of this 'martyrdom of laughter' and of his own psychological predicament is evidenced on page after page of the journals as he found himself in ever-deepening isolation and physical collapse (he died at the age of forty-two). The violence of this pain, and the belief that it was not merely accidental but was a direct result of the divine will was eloquently and frighteningly expressed in what was, dramatically enough, to be the last entry in the journal, the last words he wrote. Entitled 'The Christian Understanding of the Destiny of This Life', it is worth quoting at some length in order to show where the logic of his emphasis on suffering as the hallmark of Christian discipleship ultimately led.

> The destiny of this life is that it be brought to the extremity of life weariness. The person who when brought to that point can maintain or the person whom God helps so he is able to maintain that it is God who has brought him to that point – such a person, from the Christian point of view, passes the examination of life and is matured for eternity.

And the implications of this for our understanding of God?

> But what, specifically, does God want? He wants souls able to praise, adore, worship, and thank him – the business of angels. Therefore

God is surrounded by angels ... and what pleases him even more than the praise of angels is a human being who in the last lap of this life, when God seemingly changes into sheer cruelty and ... does everything to deprive him of all zest for life, nevertheless continues to believe that God is love, that God does it out of love. Such a human being becomes an angel ... Like a man travelling around the whole world with the fixed idea of hearing a singer with a perfect tone, God sits in heaven and listens. And every time he hears praise from a person whom he has brought to the extremity of life-weariness, God says to himself: This is it. (JP 6969)

Even if it is conceded that some strands of the Western theological tradition might logically point to such an image of 'God the cosmic torturer', it is an implication which theologians have mostly been anxious to avoid: what was it, then, that drove Kierkegaard not only to conceive such a picture of God but even, it seems, to give it credence? The vision of the world which such texts (and there are many of them in the late journals) present is one in which physical life appears as inherently and irremediably flawed, in which life in the body is almost by definition a life alienated from God, in which religion liberates us from the sickness of existence by bringing us to the point of utter world-weariness and complete contempt for the things of this world. Here Kierkegaard seems to join hands with Schopenhauer (whom he admired, albeit with reservations) in identifying Christianity with the denial of the will to life, the voluntary pursuit of extinction, a viewpoint Schopenhauer finds even more explicitly taught in Buddhism and Brahmanism. Is Kierkegaardian faith, in Freudian terms, the triumph of *thanatos* over *eros*, of the death-wish over the will to life?

These questions take us to the heart of the problematic nature of Kierkegaard's view of faith and to the heart of the psychological tragedy of his own life, where these primordial powers of life and death were embodied in two people who were of fundamental significance to him: his father, Michael Peter Kierkegaard, and the fiancée whose love he renounced, Regine Olsen. It is only by examining the dynamics of his relation to these two people that we can fully feel the force and the significance of the agonized contradiction at the very centre of his theology and spirituality. The biographical emphasis which we must now pursue does not, however, lead us away from the main path of the enquiry concerning the relation between faith and the 'age of reflection', for the conflict between Christianity and the modern spirit is intimately reflected in the circumstances of Kierkegaard's early life in a home firmly moulded in the patriarchal image.

This father, who was fifty-six when Søren was born, had himself been born a serf. He acquired his freedom in 1777 and three years later gained full citizenship. His business career was extremely successful and by 1813, the year of Søren's birth, he had become an affluent member of Copenhagen's business community and had been able to retire from active involvement in running the business (originally a hosier he had diversified into trade in a variety of commodities with China and the East Indies as well as the Danish West Indies) some years before. Despite this worldly success his character remained stamped by the impoverished feudal social and economic conditions of the Jutland Heath, where his own childhood had been spent in poverty and physical hardship. His moral and business standards bore the stamp of a strict interpretation of the Bible; his religion was sombre and pietistic. The location of the Kierkegaard household in Copenhagen's Nytorv (New Market) at the heart of the city's cultural and commercial life provided a tangible symbol of the tension between a domestic world regulated according to the unquestioned authority of this Old Testament-like patriarch and the world of an expanding mercantile city with its new-found freedoms and opportunities. Although this conflict assumed extraordinary proportions in Kierkegaard's own life, the pattern is continually repeated in the situation of modernity, as parental standards and codes are challenged by the liberties of a pluralistic society.

The ambivalence generated by such a conjunction of two diametrically opposed worlds of thought and sensibility can be seen in many aspects of Kierkegaard's life and work. As a university student he immediately and enthusiastically went the way of the world, making the most of the freedom which release from the parental home brought with it – but it was not long before guilt (and financial debt!) drove him back to the arms of the waiting father. But the most acute crisis of his life, a crisis which was in many respects to determine the actual content of his authorship, was that in which he found himself compelled to break off his engagement to his young fiancée, Regine Olsen.

The main outline of the story is simple and has been often told. In September 1840, when Søren was twenty-seven, two years after his father's death and shortly after finishing his theology degree, he became engaged to Regine, a much younger girl whom he had known for three years. Shortly after the engagement he became convinced – for reasons which Kierkegaard scholars have argued over *ad infinitum* (if not *ad nauseam*) – that it would be impossible for him to go through with it.

The following year, after completing his Master's dissertation, *On the Concept of Irony*, he broke off the engagement, an act which might not be regarded as so very exceptional today but which outraged the sensibilities of upper-middle-class Copenhagen in 1841. Two years later Regine became engaged to a former suitor whom Kierkegaard had replaced, Johan Frederik Schlegel, and was married in 1847. In 1849, on hearing of her father's death, Kierkegaard attempted to bring about a (strictly non-romantic) reconciliation but was rebuffed by Schlegel. In 1851 and 1852 it seems that she made various attempts to encounter Kierkegaard either on the streets or in church but each time he avoided responding to her advances. They last met in April 1854, shortly before she left Denmark to go with Schlegel to the Danish West Indies, where he had been appointed governor. This time they did actually speak – warmly, it seems, but briefly. When he died in 1855 Kierkegaard left her the entirety of his remaining possessions, a legacy which propriety would not allow her to accept. She later recalled that he had said to her that since in heaven there is neither marriage nor giving in marriage, she would there be able to enjoy both Schlegel and himself.

That is the external outline: what of the inner drama? It seems beyond doubt that there were strong feelings on each side, but at the same time there was something in Kierkegaard's personality which prevented him from expressing his feelings easily and spontaneously. Indeed, it was almost as if the closer he drew to another person the more he retreated into the melancholy or depression of which he once wrote: 'I say of my sorrow what the Englishman says of his home: my sorrow is my castle' (Pap. III B 179). His letters to Regine bear a painfully curious testimony to this trait: highly artificial, their convoluted rhetoric and forced metaphors are stuck together like a collage of fragments from fairy-tales and poetry books and are in no way expressive of a natural and easy passion. This is hardly surprising since, in his own words, 'the next day after the engagement I saw that I had made a mistake' (JP 6472). A key factor in this realization – whatever the psychological and biographical basis for it – was the conviction that he would be unable to confide fully in her. 'I would have had to keep too much from her, base the whole marriage on a lie' (JP 6472). In Quidam's diary in *Stages on Life's Way*, a highly autobiographical text that is also full of concealments and deceptions, he explained this psychological dilemma more fully:

And now I clearly see that my depression makes me incapable of having a confidant, and yet I know that what the marriage service

would require of me would be that she should be that. But that she
has never been, even if I had opened up as much as may be, because
we do not understand one another. That is because my consciousness goes one stop higher than hers. (SLW, p. 374)

Although Søren considered the idea of concealing this melancholy from
her, his conception of the religious obligations involved in marriage was
such that marriage would mean the complete openness of both
partners. Without this, marriage is reduced to a purely external
business, involving what he called 'the mystery system'. But

> ... the mystery system in no way leads to a happy and still less to an
> aesthetically beautiful marriage. No, my friend, candour, open-
> heartedness, revelation, understanding: this is the principle of life
> in.marriage, without it marriage is not beautiful and is essentially
> unethical ... Only when the being I live with in the fondest
> relationship known in this earthly life is in a spiritual respect as
> close as can be to me, only then is my marriage ethical and therefore
> also aesthetically beautiful. (EO 2, p. 116)

In the case of a marriage where the man wants to but cannot reveal the
essential secret of his life to his partner (Kierkegaard's own case?) the
relationship will founder in one of two ways:

> Either you will feel bound to a being who has no idea what is going
> on inside you, and your marriage then becomes an unlovely
> mésalliance. Or you tie yourself to a being who in frightful angst
> notices something and at every moment sees those shadow-pictures
> on the wall. She will, perhaps, decide never to interrogate you about
> it, never to get too near to you, she will renounce the curiosity
> aroused by her anxiety, which tempts her, but she will never be
> happy and nor will you be. (EO 2, p. 117)

What then was the secret which Kierkegaard felt unable to divulge? At
the factual level the question is perhaps insoluble. The complex,
sometimes deliberately deceptive nature of the documents does not
allow us to posit any single 'guilty event', nor can we decide with
certainty whether (if, that is, there was a single particular event at all)
this was something in Kierkegaard's own life or in the life of his father.
He once wrote that 'After my death no one will find in my papers ...
the inscription in my innermost being that interprets everything'

(JP 5645). We seem then to be faced with a blank wall. But none the less, it is clear that, whatever the facts, Kierkegaard's melancholy guilt-consciousness is grounded in his relation to his father. Most eloquent of the many testimonials to this is the journal entry called 'The Great Earthquake'.

> Then it was that the great earthquake occurred, the frightful upheaval which suddenly drove me to a new infallible principle for interpreting all the phenomena. Then I surmised that my father's old age was not a divine blessing, but rather a curse, that our family's exceptional intellectual capacities were only for mutually harrowing one another; then I felt the stillness of death deepen around me, when I saw in my father an unhappy man who would survive us all, a memorial cross on the grave of all his personal hopes. A guilt must rest upon the entire family, a punishment of God must be upon it: it was supposed to disappear, obliterated by the mighty hand of God, erased like a mistake ... (JP 5430)

Here as elsewhere we see a clear correlation between the figure of the elder Kierkegaard and the themes of death, guilt and sexuality in the writings of his son. Birth itself is, for Kierkegaard, a guilty act: 'I came into existence through a crime, I came into existence against God's will' (JP 6969). It is perhaps not insignificant that the Danish theological term for 'original sin' means literally 'inherited sin', and it is not stretching the image too far to say that the world-denying model of faith which came so to dominate Søren's view of Christianity was indeed an inheritance from his father. It is a reiteration of the Christianity which he regarded as the Christianity of this father, and indeed he could quite explicitly declare that his father according to the flesh was also for him his father in God. 'How I thank you, Father in heaven,' he wrote, 'for having kept an earthly father present for a time here on earth, where I so greatly need him; with your help I hope that he will have greater joy in being my father the second time than he had the first time' (JP 5328). Ultimately the distinction between this earthly father, who became his father 'a second time' when the son turned back to Christianity, and the heavenly father is (at least in psychological terms) more than a little blurred. Kierkegaard himself wrote that it came 'so naturally' to him to speak to God as to his father (JP 6645). The consequences of his earthly father becoming his father 'a second time' were spelled out in a journal entry dated on the same day (9 July 1838):

> I am going to work toward a far more inward relation to Christianity, for up until now I have in a way been standing completely outside it while fighting for its truth; like Simon of Cyrene (Luke 23.26) I have carried Christ's cross in a purely external way. (JP 5329)

It was this resolve to take up the cross in a radical and inward way that led to the religious abyss of that final devastating entry in the journal, and it was a resolve that issued from his submission to the will of the father. It was this father who, spiritually if not literally, had held before his child the image of the crucified one, an image which came to haunt the grown man with the demand that he should suffer similarly, a demand which Kierkegaard likened to the guilty conscience of a murderer. By his birth the son had diminished the father's life, a crime for which he would have to pay by sacrificing his own life and happiness.

As far as the bulk of the authorship is concerned, it was not the living father whom Kierkegaard sought to propitiate but the dead father, or more precisely, the memory of the deceased father. 'Most precious of all that I have inherited from him is his memory, his transfigured image . . .' (JP 5335), he wrote. It was this transfigured image of a man who had once been seen by the son as a cross on the grave of his descendants which became for Kierkegaard the symbol of eternity and of its demands on the world of time. Nor is this merely fanciful psychologizing. At the theoretical level Kierkegaard himself finds in our relation to the dead the key by which to reverse the values of 'nineteenth-century rational man'. In one of the most beautiful entries in the early journals he describes a moment of intense communion with the 'dear departed ones' who fill his thoughts as he wanders on the lonely cliff-tops of northern Sjaelland.

> I was very much at ease in their midst, I rested in their embrace, and I felt as if transported out of my body and floating about with them in a higher ether – but then the seagull's harsh screech reminded me that I stood alone, and everything vanished before my eyes, and I turned back with a heavy heart to mingle with the world's crowds . . . (JP 5099)

The opposition between the quiet communion with the transfigured memory of the dead and the noise of the crowd is strongly drawn and the full theological implications of this are made explicit in *Purity of Heart* where Kierkegaard describes how such communion with the dead can serve to deliver the individual from his immersion in the busy world of modern-day life.

> Or if one of those distinguished men, whose memory the crowd keeps fresh with noisy festivities and shouting, as befits the crowd, what if he (which is much more serious) should come to you and visit you: would you then dare to continue in your occupation beneath his penetrating gaze? Even if you are not familiar with such thoughts it could well be that it is in such a way that these transfigured ones might wish to be of service after their death ... the transfigured one, like eternity, does not want the crowd, he wants the individual. (UDVS, p. 138)

The term 'transfigure' occurs frequently at key moments in Kierkegaard's authorship. In the aesthetics of his day it referred to the transfiguration of material form by ideal truth, the visible illumination of the natural and human world by the world of ideas. Similarly Kierkegaard could, as we have seen, speak of the individual life being transfigured by the divine presence when it becomes pure and transparent to its own divine ground. Here, however, the union of the divine and human which the concept of transfiguration points to is transferred from the sphere of concrete worldly existence to the world of the dead. Now, it seems, it is only the dead who, while in some sense remaining human, can also possess the decisive attribute of divine being: eternity. Like God, the dead do not change, and so the dead become the bridgehead between the human world of change and decay and the divine world of unchanging eternity.

> But take care with the dead! For the dead man is finished and definite; he is not like we others still in search of adventure ... When you say to a dead man, 'I shall never forget you,' it is as if he answered 'Good: and you can be sure that I shall never forget that you have said it.' And even if all your contemporaries were to assure you that he has forgotten it: you will never hear this from the mouth of the dead man himself. No, he goes to his place – but he is not changed ... A dead man, even if you do not notice it in him, is a strong man: he has the strength of unchangeableness. (WL, pp. 356–7)

Our relation to the dead is also placed at the pinnacle of the schema of possible forms of love set out in *Works of Love*. Our love for the dead,

Kierkegaard argues, is the most disinterested, the freest and the most faithful form of love. 'Truly, if you want to assure yourself as to the love that is in you, or in another man, pay attention to how he behaves towards the dead' (WL, p. 347).

In its most extreme form the unchanging demand made on us by the dead is that we, like them, die to the world. The duty of honouring the dead slides into the wish to identify and to be identified with them, a wish betrayed by Kierkegaard in a journal entry he wrote on a pilgrimage to (not insignificantly!) his father's birthplace at Saeding in Jutland. 'I sit here all alone ... and count the hours until I shall see Saeding ... What if I were to get sick and be buried in the Saeding churchyard! What a strange idea! ... is this actually to be the sum and substance of my life?' (JP 5468). What a strange idea indeed – but quite comprehensible in terms of Kierkegaard's own logic. Was it then the sum and substance of his life to be surrendered up to the will of the dead father, to this dead and death-demanding father to whom he sacrificed the lively and potentially life-creating relationship to the girl he saw as a symbol of the joyous immediacy of life and of his own possibility of participating in such immediacy? In this question we can see how the engagement crisis epitomized the conflict between the living and the dead, between the world of the crowd and the world of the solitary individual, between love and death, *eros* and *thanatos*, a conflict that was central both to Kierkegaard the man and Kierkegaard the writer. In an entry written some time before the engagement Kierkegaard himself expressed the conflict in almost these very terms:

> You blind god of erotic love! You who see in secret, will you disclose it to me? Will I experience the conclusion of all my life's eccentric premisses, will I fold you in my arms, or: Do The Orders say: March On? Have you gone on ahead, you, my longing, transfigured do you beckon to me from another world? O, I will throw everything away to become light enough to follow you. (JP 5368)

It is a stark choice: between the fulfilment of erotic passion in this life and the fulfilment of a sublimated and 'transfigured' longing in 'another world'. Once more the conflict is mirrored in Quidam's diary when the diarist confesses to the belief that if he had married his young lady he would have stood beside her on the wedding-day with the thought that one of them must die before night (SLW, p. 375). Kierkegaard's tragic outlook scarcely dared to envisage the real possibility for him of a happy union between the religious demand enshrined in the marriage ceremony and the sensuous passion of the wedding-night. The moment of erotic fulfilment is haunted and thwarted by the omnipresent and remorseless will-to-death. Kierkegaard used the story of Abraham and Isaac to interpret the renunciation he made in giving up the happiness of married life, but the image is perhaps also significant in a way he did not fully intend. For he not only sacrificed Regine, he also sacrificed himself: he was the Isaac deprived of life through the dark and inexplicably guilty God-consciousness of the father. In addition, this story was for Kierkegaard, as for the ancient typological interpreters of the Bible, also a 'type' of the sacrifice of the cross. The radical discipleship of the crucified one was thus a consistent extension of the self-sacrifice of the son to the impenetrable will of the father.

Kierkegaard's submission to this will was not made without a struggle, however. The will to life, the will to deny the denial of the will-to-live, also appears abundantly in his work. 'If I had had faith, I would have stayed with Regine' (JP 5664), he wrote in 1843. Faith here does not mean the sacrifice of life but the paradoxical breakthrough of the spirit to life, the double-movement of renunciation that leads to affirmation. The blocking of the flow of life is seen in this perspective as 'shut-upness' and described as demoniacal, and we can see Kierkegaard struggling against such 'shut-upness' throughout his life, a shut-upness which echoed the loneliness of a child shut up in the gloomy patriarchal home while outside in the market-place the world laughed and played in the sunshine.

In one moment of jubilation, on the Wednesday of Holy Week, 1848, he wrote: 'My whole nature is changed. My concealment and inclosing reserve, i.e. shut-upness are broken – I am free to speak' (JP 6131). On Easter Monday, however: 'No, no, my inclosing reserve still cannot be broken ...' (JP 6133). The engagement itself, undertaken it should be noted after the 'Great Earthquake' and after the father's death, represents another, quickly frustrated movement of the will to life. 'In the purely human sense it signified for me ... my salvation. But I could not enter that harbor. I was to be used in another way' (JP 6473). He was, then, unable to bring the psychological powers of his mental constitution into harmony, unable to achieve the synthesis of the polarities of being which he himself had defined as the hallmark of authentic selfhood. His was a divided self: 'For many years my depression has prevented me from saying "Du" to myself in the profoundest sense' (JP 5980). A man at war with himself, Kierkegaard's psyche was the battleground of two hostile primordial powers, two worlds that could not be reconciled, and that reduced him to a state of utter world-weariness, a case of what the psychiatrist Karl Menninger was to call 'chronic suicide'.[2] In this perspective it must seem that Kierkegaard is very poorly qualified to act as a doctor for the sickness of the modern world: is it not one of the achievements of the twentieth century that it can offer a cure for this kind of religious 'morbidity'? Do we not have a science (psycho-analysis) which can unlock the mystery of the hidden conflicts between instinct and authority which torment the lives of such 'cases' as Søren Kierkegaard? Far from the modern age needing Kierkegaard, it might seem that the opposite is the case: he was one who desperately needed the psycho-sexual liberation which the modern world has made possible.

But what if it is in his very suffering, in his failure to overcome his divided self, that Kierkegaard matters most to us? In a magisterial study the Scandinavian scholar Eduard Geismar once tried to distinguish between the morbid and the healthy elements in Kierkegaard's work, to separate out the wheat from the tares. Yet this is an impossible task, for it is Kierkegaard's psychological failure itself which shows us just what is at stake in the struggle for selfhood. It may be said of him what Thomas Mann said of Schopenhauer: 'His pessimism – that is his humanity.'[3] For what the 'morbid' side of Kierkegaard's work – his 'dark shadow' to use a term from Jungian psychology – reveals is the passion that dares to break out of the mediocrity and banality of a conformist society. As well as the truth of the comfortable majority there is also a kind of truth which speaks from the sidelines of society, a truth which though disturbing should not be simply ignored.

> The busy ones, who neither labour nor are heavy laden, but are merely busy, think that they have escaped if in this life they have avoided suffering, and so they don't want to be disturbed by hearing or thinking about anything frightening. Yes, certainly they have escaped having any view of life, and escaped into meaninglessness. (UDVS, pp. 106–7)

But the realm of alternative meanings (whether or not we share the particular alternative which Kierkegaard made his own) is one in which the risk of personal and psychological shipwreck is inevitably high, and this will be all the more true the more society is able to rationalize and organize the arousal and satisfaction of human needs. The more successful the society, the more lonely the deviant.

It is also true that one who puts himself outside the norm and excludes himself from the majority, will, sooner or later, encounter hostility and rejection, however politely that may be expressed.[4] Kierkegaard's suffering gave him a standpoint from which to see into the fundamental dynamics of the relationship between society and its outsiders, and to see that the existence of such outsiders, of such alternative viewpoints, means that we cannot foreclose on all the possibilities of human life by mindlessly adopting the prevailing philosophy of our society. These other perspectives must at the very least be taken into account.

Max Horkheimer, a leading proponent of 'critical theory', wrote that it was the task of religion

> ... to make man conscious that he is a finite being, that he must suffer and die; that beyond suffering and death there is a longing that this earthly being may not be absolute or final ... In the concept of God the idea was for a long time preserved that there are other criteria for evaluating life than those expressed by the efficient working of nature and society.[5]

In this way Kierkegaard's other-worldliness has a humanistic edge: it is a reminder that the horizon of humanity can never be closed, that the 'success' of bourgeois society does not totally extinguish the 'longing for the wholly other' (Horkheimer), and that it is only by pitting ourselves against the absolute frontier of eternity that we will be able to discover who we really are in our capacity for both love and death, darkness and light.

The biographical contextualization of Kierkegaardian melancholy is highly relevant to the question as to the relationship between Kierkegaard's thought and the philosophy of dialogue of Buber, Gabriel Marcel and Mikhail Bakhtin. For the struggle to unify the conflicting polarities of the self as Kierkegaard represents it is not simply a struggle between two reified powers or abstract principles: it is at its heart a struggle shaped by the presence in his writing of the two actual people, the old man and the young woman, whose life-stories are so intertwined with those of Søren himself that even the briefest summaries of his thought mention them. Kierkegaard's religious struggle is never separable from the struggle to discover and to live out the unconditional obligation of love in the context of these most intimate relationships. I have used the term 'individuation' in this study and should therefore note here that there is an important limit to the usefulness of this term. The story of the self told by Kierkegaard is a story of individuation – but it would be more correct to say that it is a drama of individuation, a drama of how to be myself in face of the other who confronts and constrains me and by doing so requires me to become who I really am.

In theological terms Kierkegaard's understanding of what was involved in the imitation of Christ may be extreme. But if his doctrine of the cross threatens to tear itself away from its doctrinal base in the incarnation and in creation, if the demand of the cross came to oppose and eventually replace the journey to selfhood as the main focus of Kierkegaard's understanding of Christian spirituality, we should not dismiss all talk of the cross or of imitation as unhealthy. What is not true in isolation may have its place in the overall economy of the religious life. Kierkegaard often claimed that he was only a 'corrective', a deliberately one-sided balance to the worldliness of contemporary religion. Nietzsche and Freud have made us suspicious of those who seek out suffering for themselves, but it may be that, within the context of a good creation and in relation to the hallowing of that creation by the incarnation, there can on occasion sound a call to suffering and radical discipleship which is quite distinct from the resentments of sadism and masochism. If we cannot endorse all that Kierkegaard says on these subjects, we can still read it and still learn from it.

EIGHT

INCONCLUSIVE UNSCIENTIFIC POSTSCRIPT

———

THIS STUDY OF Kierkegaard's thought took as its starting-point the crisis of faith as focused by the debate about non-realism in contemporary British theology. However, the picture of Kierkegaard that has emerged does not seem to provide any obvious 'answer' to that debate. Not only does the complex entanglement of his thought with the circumstances of his own life seem to render him remote from our agenda, but the idiosyncratic content of both life and thought seem to cry out for the therapeutic application of postmodernity's life-affirming insights. Even if Kierkegaard's critique of objectivity might justify including him in the family-tree of revisionist theologies, the content of his personal faith – adoring surrender to God the cosmic torturer – seems to identify him with all those aspects of religion that postmodern believers are duty-bound to reject. Has Kierkegaard, then, become a figure of purely historical interest? Or is there still a sense in which Kierkegaard is our contemporary?

I have noted that, consistent with the emphasis on subjectivity in his theoretical work, Kierkegaard's writing again and again reveals its interconnection with the struggle to make sense of his own personal life and circumstances. This very interconnection exemplifies the logic of self-involvement that has characterized Christian writing from Paul, through Augustine, Luther, Bunyan and beyond. Christian theology is, in principle, inseparable from the story of the believing-yet-unbelieving self, seeking faith and attempting to practise the works of faith. Whether this is understood individualistically or, as in much contemporary theology, more collectively, it radically destabilizes the whole venture of theology, if that is held to be the objective unfolding of a fixed body of timelessly true doctrines. That which is believed is meaningless apart from those who believe it.

This not only means that every significant work of theology acquires an autobiographical dimension. Although that is a not unimportant rule-of-thumb that theologians are all too prone to forget, it is not the main point. For Kierkegaard's understanding of subjectivity and his practice as a writer pose a still more fundamental question: Do we in fact know what it is for the self to be a self? If the autobiographical character of theology is understood in such a way as to assume that we all already know what a person is, what belongs to the essence of their life and life-story, and that we can explain the theology by simply cross-referencing the life, then we still have not grasped Kierkegaard's full significance in this respect. The point is not that the theory represents the life but that the life is itself called into question by the questions to which the theory is addressed *and that this calling-into-question is a continuing condition of being able to formulate the fundamental questions of theology.*

This has an important implication for the evaluation of revisionist theologies. It is true that in a work such as *Life Lines*[1] Don Cupitt acknowledges the interconnectedness of theology and personal life. On the other hand, the rhetoric of much revisionist theology suggests a quasi-Hegelian understanding of the history of ideas, as if we are now standing on some kind of assured vantage-point that enables us to make definitive judgements as to the meaning of all previous theologies and philosophies of life, as if we can see their meaning in a manner that was closed to those who wrote them and lived them first hand. Now it is true that new perspectives emerge in the course of history and new readings bring old works to life in fresh and often startling ways. None the less, such perspectives as we have are never enough for us to impose any kind of closure on historical material as long as we ourselves live in, with and under the temporal and subjective conditions of historical existence. Because we put the meaning of our own lives at stake in every venture of interpretation, and because that stake is always exposed to loss, gain or redefinition in every game, the kind of certitude demonstrated by many revisionist theologies as to what is or is not theologically valid just is not possible. This lesson we can learn from Kierkegaard, and, having learned it, we will be committed to a generous and open approach to the religious tradition and to the plurality of religious points of view represented among our contemporaries. When revisionists declare that modern or postmodern believers cannot believe this or that doctrine because of its scientific impossibility or cultural irrelevance, they sometimes display a lack of self-questioning that can slip into the kind of brash self-assurance of nineteenth-century materialistic humanism as exemplified by the early Feuerbach or by Nietzsche at his worst. Such assertions lead in any case to a foreshortening of interpretative horizons and to the impoverishment of the resources of religious living. The one thing we can rule out in advance is that there is nothing that can be ruled out in advance. Again and again, as it has throughout history, religion will renew itself from the encounter with what is strange and unexpected in the past no less than it will have to redefine itself in relation to the new.

It may seem then as if Kierkegaard is to be enlisted among the defenders of so-called traditionalism, in so far as he seems to join traditionalists in accusing radicals of theological hubris. However, it is important to note that, on his lips, this charge is not made in the name of any unquestioned principle of authority but in the name of the radical questionability of the self whose voice is heard in all theological assertion and counter-assertion. If revisionists exemplify one kind of closure, the standpoint of traditionalism (in its ecclesiastically conservative form) makes closure the very principle of its existence. This is not because of its often justifiable defence of the content of certain doctrinal positions, but because of the way in which it translates existential questions into the language of diplomacy and the committee-room and its presupposing of a consensual community in the face of questions that call the very existence of such a community into doubt. The 'we' of 'we moderns' who can no longer believe as our forebears once believed and the 'we' of the traditionalist who speaks only on behalf of the 'we' of the Church are equally suspect to those who have felt the tremors of Kierkegaardian subjectivity.

Does what has just been said imply that, even if he cannot be pressed into the specific mould of the postmodern paradigm, Kierkegaard's thought leads, none the less, to some kind of relativism, whereby all views are equally valid if believed with sufficient enthusiasm and commitment?

It certainly is the case that the Kierkegaardian principle of subjectivity does restrain us from pre-emptive judgements as to the truth or value of particular assertions until we have attended to them with the kind of focus and intensity that is needed to elicit their subjective value. I must approach each expression of another's point of view with the respect that comes from understanding that the subjectivity of others is just as important to them as mine is to me, their future just as interesting to them as mine to me, their freedom just as unfathomable and frightening as I experience mine to be. If freedom is the magic lamp from which the spirit appears I must face the truth that each one of us can only rub it for themselves. The universality of metaphysics collapses into the void of 'angst' in which and through which each must make their own way. I cannot legislate for how others must negotiate this difficult journey.

But this is not the same as saying that all views are equally valid, and it is very different from the kind of relativism that assumes the standpoint of a detached, scientific spectator.

The principle of subjectivity may problematize many of the traditional criteria by which truth and falsehood are distinguished in discourse about religion, but it is not itself without criteria of any kind. It is possible – although not without the discipline of patient and careful reading – to distinguish between the important and the trivial, the abiding and the ephemeral, the edifying and the merely entertaining, even if we simultaneously acknowledge that many or all of the judgements we make in such matters will themselves be open to question and revision.

But how far do such criteria reach? Kierkegaard's Seducer took as the leitmotif of his philosophy of life the Romantic concept of 'the interesting'. Renouncing the idea that it was possible to have a complete, exhaustive understanding of the true nature of things à la Hegel, the Romantics believed that works of nature, poetry or art commended themselves to us on the basis of their being interesting, showing only one aspect or facet of their being to us but doing so in such a way as to lure us on to a further involvement and investigation. Thus, an 'interesting' person (in this technical sense) is someone in whom we guess there to be more than meets the eye, someone whose conversation hints at knowledge or experiences that they never openly discuss – and our curiosity is aroused, we want to know more, we are intrigued, 'interested'. Do the kind of criteria that Kierkegaardian subjectivity allows for perhaps amount to no more than this: that they help us to identify what works, what authors, what topics are 'interesting' for contemporary study?

Let us not dismiss the question too quickly. What makes the Seducer's private cult of 'the interesting' depraved is the way in which he takes up an attitude of non-involved spectatorship towards the objects of his 'interest' and refuses to put himself at risk in the pseudo-relationships that he creates. But what if we were to graft on to the Romantic concept of 'the interesting' the concept of interest developed by Kierkegaard in the *Concluding Unscientific Postscript*? That concept, it will be recalled, meant precisely the necessary involvement of the self in the question at issue. As such Kierkegaard regarded it as the opposite of all a priori metaphysical thinking and as pre-eminently appropriate for thinking about questions of faith. Putting the two aspects of 'the interesting' together, then, we can say that a religious text, author or idea is interesting to the degree that it invites further and continuing exploration (the most interesting being what promises inexhaustible scope for interpretation and application) *and* requires us to see the meaning and value of our own existence being at stake in it ('our own' comprising not only myself as an isolated ego, but also my neighbour as one whose meaning and value is likewise at issue in questions of religious truth).

To take an example: much catechetical material is essentially uninteresting in this sense because although it notionally answers to one half of our requirement – the issues at stake in right belief are claimed to be of ultimate concern – the material is necessarily presented in such a way as to define and to constrain the process of ongoing and open enquiry. Its correctness means that what you see is all you get. There are and can be no hidden dimensions to lure or excite further ventures of interpretation. The canon of religious classics constructed on the basis of our Kierkegaardian concept of 'the interesting' will, on the other hand, be works that continually require further interpretation and that simultaneously engage the greatest manifold of our concerns in an open and unresolved dialogue with the matter under discussion. Such works will reflect a wide and deep acquaintance with the historical and cultural conditions of their production and yet will not be mere reflections of contemporary cultural trends; they will be works that reach after questions, concepts and ideas that have proved their power to transcend narrow cultural boundaries by being constantly taken up anew in the ongoing life of the tradition and in a significant variety of cultural contexts; they will be works that lead us into the depths of our communal, psychological and personal struggles for meaningful life; they will be works in which religion takes on human flesh and draws near to us while yet preserving its startling strangeness.

Perhaps these criteria could be more finely tuned. Perhaps the very notion of canon is challengeable, and certainly any canon arrived at will remain open to debate. (Even the canon of scripture remains, after all, a matter of contention between Jewish, Roman Catholic, Orthodox and Protestant communities!) Notwithstanding all such qualifications, however, I believe that we are able to make judgements as to what might be included or excluded, and that these judgements are not the exercise of arbitrary subjectivism. Few would want to deny Augustine, Dante, Luther or Julian of Norwich the accolade of 'classic status' defined in these terms. They are all prime examples of Christian writers thoroughly rooted in their time and place whose exploration of personal meaning is simultaneously an exposition of the psychological, cultural and metaphysical conditions of meaning. In the utter singularity of their self-commitment they reach out towards universality. In reading what mattered to them, we learn more of what matters (or could or even should) matter to us. Even when their cultural situation or psychological crises make them unassimilable in their own terms or when we cannot share their metaphysical assumptions, they remain figures who shape what it is for human beings, living in history, to be religious. As such they are also able to speak beyond the community of faith, as Kierkegaard spoke to Sartre, the Marxist atheist, who could write of him that 'Reading Kierkegaard I reascend back to myself; I seek to grasp Kierkegaard and it is myself I hold ... Each of us *is* Soeren in our capacity as adventure.'[2] Sartre thus strengthens my conviction that despite the unique problems of reading Kierkegaard, his work not only helps us to redefine the nature of the theological canon, but itself belongs within the canon of Christian classics. It not only reacted to but helped to define some of the key questions of modernity in the spheres of philosophy, culture and political life; it reinterpreted and made available for modernity the inheritance of radical Christian piety; and it tracked both cultural and religious questions into the primal landscapes of the psychic struggle for wholeness and purpose. As a modern classic, Kierkegaard's work deserves to be read and reread by each Christian generation in its search for the self-understanding of faith, a search that in each of us individually as in the Christian community as a whole seeks resources from the past as it reaches towards the future.

Kierkegaard will appear revolutionary, negative and corrosive to those who experience (or imagine that they experience) the religious tradition as being still largely intact. That is how he was seen by many in his own time. In our age such a position is much harder to maintain. God is, if not dead, in fragments, and with God much of the doctrinal and moral teaching of religion. In such a situation Kierkegaardian individualism need no longer be a sign of dissolution and decay: it has the possibility of feeding the new beginnings of faith and shaping the new contexts in which God will be thought about and spoken about and the religious life practised. Understood in this way, Kierkegaard is indeed our contemporary.

Notes

1 Kierkegaard and the Crisis of Faith

1 D. Cupitt, *The Sea of Faith: Christianity in Change*. London, BBC, 1984.
2 Quoted in C. L. Creegan, *Wittgenstein and Kierkegaard*. London, Routledge, 1989, p. 18.
3 P. Tillich, *Theology of Culture*. London and New York, OUP, 1959, p. 108.
4 W. Lowrie, 'Introduction' in S. Kierkegaard, *Stages on Life's Way*. London and New York, OUP, 1940, p. 13.
5 P. Mesnard, *Le Vrai Visage de Kierkegaard*. Paris, Beauchesne, 1948, p. 265.
6 R. Friedman, *Kierkegaard: The Analysis of the Psychological Personality*. London, Peter Nevill, 1949, p. 47.
7 F. Nietzsche, *The Will to Power*. New York, Vintage, 1968, p. 9.
8 R. Bultmann, *History and Eschatology*. Edinburgh, Edinburgh University Press, 1957, pp. 10–11.
9 A. Storr (ed.), *Jung: Selected Writings*. London, Fontana, 1983, p. 392.
10 D. Cupitt, *Taking Leave of God*. London, SCM, 1984, p. 94.
11 Cupitt, *Taking Leave of God*, p. 94.
12 Cupitt, *Taking Leave of God*, p. 5.
13 Cupitt, *Taking Leave of God*, p. 9.
14 Cupitt, *Taking Leave of God*, p. 96.

2 Critique of the Age

1 F. Schiller, *Letters on the Aesthetic Education of Man*. Oxford, OUP, 1967, pp. 33–5.
2 P. M. Møller, *Efterladte Skrifter*, vol. 5. Copenhagen, Reitzel, 1856, p. 41.
3 Møller, *Efterladte Skrifter*, vol. 1, p. 134.
4 C. G. Jung (ed.), *Man and His Symbols*. London, Aldus, 1964, p. 95.
5 In Jung, *Man and His Symbols*, p. 212.
6 J. Henry, 'The Term "Primitive" in Kierkegaard and Heidegger', in A. Montagu (ed.), *The Concept of the Primitive*. New York, Free Press, 1968, p. 220.
7 W. Kasper, *Jesus the Christ*. London, Burns & Oates, 1977, p. 16.
8 H. L. Martensen, 'Fata Morgana af J. L. Heiberg', in *Maanedskrift for Literatur*, 19, 1838, p. 367.

3 Critique of Society

1 B. Kirmmse, *Kierkegaard in Golden Age Denmark*. Bloomington, Indiana University Press, 1990, p. 275.
2 E. Brunner and K. Barth, *Natural Theology*. London, Geoffrey Bles, 1946, p. 30.
3 See B. Bertung, *Om Kierkegaard, Kvinder og Kærlighed* [On Kierkegaard, Women and Love]. Copenhagen, Reitzel, 1987.
4 D. Sölle, 'Angst und Glauben', in *Kierkegaardiana*, 13, 1984. See also Wanda Warren Berry, 'Kierkegaard and Feminism: Apologetic, Repetition and Dialogue', in M. Matustik and M. Westphal (eds), *Kierkegaard in Post/Modernity*. Bloomington, Indiana University Press, 1994.
5 D. Bonhoeffer, *The Cost of Discipleship*. London, SCM, 1959, p. 273.

4 Critique of Philosophy and Science

1 G. W. F. Hegel, *The Phenomenology of Spirit*. Oxford, OUP, 1979, p. 11.
2 Hegel, *Phenomenology of Spirit*, p. 3.
3 See, for example, the essays 'The Question Concerning Technology' and 'The Age of the World Picture' in M. Heidegger, *The Question Concerning Technology*. New York, Harper & Row, 1977.
4 R. Descartes, *Discourse on Method*. Harmondsworth, Penguin Classics, 1968, p. 53.
5 Hegel, *Phenomenology of Spirit*, p. 49.
6 Hegel, *Phenomenology of Spirit*, p. 50.
7 A. Trendelenburg, *Logische Untersuchungen*. Berlin, 1840, p. 5.
8 Trendelenburg, *Logische Untersuchungen*, p. 25.
9 Trendelenburg, *Logische Untersuchungen*, p. 41.
10 J.-P. Sartre, *Between Existentialism and Marxism*. London, NLB, 1974, p. 157.
11 A. Schweitzer, *Civilization and Ethics*. London, Unwin, 1961, p. 185.

5 Critique of Art

1 A. Fallico, *Art and Existentialism*. New Jersey, Prentice-Hall, 1962, p. 83.
2 F. Nietzsche, *The Will to Power*. New York, Vintage, 1967, p. 453.
3 Nietzsche, *Will to Power*, p. 452.
4 H. Steffens, *Inledninger til Philosophiske Forelæsninger i København* (1803). Copenhagen, Gyldendal, 1905, p. 22.
5 S. T. Coleridge, *Biographia Literaria*. London, Everyman, 1906, p. 166.
6 H. Marcuse, *An Essay on Liberation*. Harmondsworth, Penguin, 1969, p. 38.
7 M. Warnock, 'Imagination – Aesthetic and Religious', in *Theology*, LXXXIII, 1980, p. 408.

8 From H. Heine, 'Lass die heil'gen Parabolen', in *Sämtliche Werke*, vol. II. Münich, Ros, 1923, p. 410.

9 P. M. Møller, *Efterladte Skrifter*, vol. 3. Copenhagen, Reitzel, p. 160.

10 See G. Pattison, *Art, Modernity and Faith*. Basingstoke, Macmillan, 1991, pp. 115–17.

11 G. Abrahams, *The Concise Oxford History of Music*. Oxford, OUP, 1979, p. 821.

12 H. Küng, *Art and the Question of Meaning*. London, SCM, 1981, p. 12.

13 G. W. F. Hegel, *Aesthetics. Lectures on Fine Art*. Oxford, OUP, 1975, pp. 9–10, 11.

14 See Pattison, *Art, Modernity and Faith*, especially ch. 6.

15 D. Cupitt, *Taking Leave of God*. London, SCM, 1980, pp. 69–70.

6 Becoming an Individual

1 See K. Nordentoft, *Hvad Siger Brand-Majoren?* [What Does the Fire-Chief Say?]. Copenhagen, Gad, 1973, pp. 112–14. See also, B. Kirmmse, *Kierkegaard in Golden Age Denmark*, Bloomington, Indiana University Press, pp. 273–8.

2 M. Buber, *Between Man and Man*. London, Fontana, 1961, p. 63. See also the essays by Andic, George and Pyper in G. Pattison and S. Shakespeare (eds), *Kierkegaard: The Self in Society*. Basingstoke, Macmillan, 1997.

3 Buber, *Between Man and Man*, p. 71.

4 Buber, *Between Man and Man*, p. 79.

5 Buber, *Between Man and Man*, p. 89.

6 Buber, *Between Man and Man*, pp. 31–2.

7 Doctor or Patient?

1 See H. Fenger, *Kierkegaard. The Myths and their Origins*. New Haven and London, Yale University Press, 1980.

2 See K. Menninger, *Man Against Himself*. New York, Harvest, 1938.

3 T. Mann in *The Living Thoughts of Schopenhauer*. London, Cassell, 1939.

4 There is in this respect much in Kierkegaard's work that illustrates the theory of scapegoating put forward by René Girard. See, for example, D. McCracken, *The Scandal of the Gospels*. New York, OUP, 1994.

5 M. Horkheimer, *Der Sehnsucht nach dem Ganz Anderen*. Hamburg, Furche, 1970, p. 67. See also a recent study of the significance of Kierkegaardian melancholy as a principle by which to critique modernity and postmodernity: H. Ferguson, *Melancholy and the Critique of Modernity*. London, Routledge, 1995.

8 Inconclusive Unscientific Postscript

1 Don Cupitt, *Life Lines*. London, SCM, 1986.
2 J.-P. Sartre, *Between Existentialism and Marxism*. London, Verso, 1974.

Suggestions for Further Reading

Biographical

The best English-language survey of the intellectual and cultural background of Kierkegaard's life and times is Bruce Kirmmse, *Kierkegaard in Golden Age Denmark*, Bloomington, Indiana University Press, 1990. Bruce Kirmmse's *Encounters with Kierkegaard: A Life as Seen by His Contemporaries*, Princeton University Press, 1996, is invaluable in collating all known contemporary accounts of Kierkegaard's personality. Other useful biographical materials are to be found in S. Kierkegaard (tr. Rosenmeier), *Letters and Documents*, Princeton University Press, 1978, and in S. Kierkegaard (tr. and ed. Howard V. and Edna H. Hong), *The Corsair Affair*, Princeton University Press, 1982. There is no good recent biography in English, and many of the older biographies are extremely tendentious. However, the basic facts are assembled in Walter Lowrie, *A Short Life of Kierkegaard*, Princeton University Press, 1942 & 1970.

Theology and Philosophy

The secondary literature on Kierkegaard is enormous, but the following is a representative sample of good recent works in English:

C. Stephen Evans, *Passionate Reason: Making Sense of Kierkegaard's Fragments*. Bloomington, Indiana University Press, 1992.

Peter Fenves, *'Chatter': Language and History in Kierkegaard*. Stanford University Press, 1993.

Harvie Ferguson, *Melancholy and the Critique of Modernity*. London, Routledge, 1995.

M. Jamie Ferreira, *Transforming Vision: Imagination and Will in Kierkegaardian Faith*. Oxford, Clarendon Press, 1991.

David Gouwens, *Kierkegaard as Religious Thinker*. Cambridge University Press, 1996.

Alastair Hannay, *Kierkegaard*. London, Routledge, 1982.

David Law, *Kierkegaard as Negative Theologian*. Oxford, Clarendon Press, 1993.

John Douglas Mullen, *Kierkegaard's Philosophy: Self-Deception and Cowardice in the Present Age*. New York, New American Library, 1981.

George Pattison, *Kierkegaard: The Aesthetic and the Religious*. Basingstoke, Macmillan, 1992.

Anthony Rudd, *Kierkegaard and the Limits of the Ethical*. Oxford, Clarendon Press, 1993.

Sylvia Walsh, *Living Poetically: Kierkegaard's Existential Aesthetics*. Pennsylvania University Press, 1994.

Julia Watkin, *Kierkegaard*. London, Chapman, 1997.

Michael Weston, *Kierkegaard and Modern Continental Philosophy*. London, Routledge, 1994.

Also useful for a more specialist approach are the journal *Kierkegaardiana* and the continuing series edited by Robert L. Perkins and published by Macon University Press: *International Kierkegaard Commentary*, with a volume dedicated to each of the volumes in Princeton's complete edition of *Kierkegaard's Writings*. The Howard and Edna Hong Kierkegaard Library at St Olaf College, Minnesota, publishes a regular Newsletter and, with the Søren Kierkegaard Research Centre in Copenhagen University, is a major resource and contact point for those wishing to research Kierkegaard's work in depth.

INDEX

The Society for Promoting Christian Knowledge (SPCK) has as its purpose three main tasks:

- **Communicating the Christian faith in its rich diversity**
- **Helping people to understand the Christian faith and to develop their personal faith**
- **Equipping Christians for mission and ministry**

SPCK Worldwide serves the Church through Christian literature and communication projects in over 100 countries. Special schemes also provide books for those training for ministry in many parts of the developing world. SPCK Worldwide's ministry involves Churches of many traditions. This worldwide service depends upon the generosity of others and all gifts are spent wholly on ministry programmes, without deductions.

SPCK Bookshops support the life of the Christian community by making available a full range of Christian literature and other resources, and by providing support to bookstalls and book agents throughout the UK. SPCK Bookshops' mail order department meets the needs of overseas customers and those unable to have access to local bookshops.

SPCK Publishing produces Christian books and resources, covering a wide range of inspirational, pastoral, practical and academic subjects. Authors are drawn from many different Christian traditions, and publications aim to meet the needs of a wide variety of readers in the UK and throughout the world.

The Society does not necessarily endorse the individual views contained in its publications, but hopes they stimulate readers to think about and further develop their Christian faith.

For further information about the Society, please write to:
SPCK, Holy Trinity Church, Marylebone Road,
London NW1 4DU, United Kingdom.
Telephone: 0171 387 5282